THE SPARK

THE SPARK

IT'S WHAT THEY WANT

J. La Tulippe

1603 Capitol Ave., Suite 310 Cheyenne, Wyoming USA 82001
1-888-980-6523 | admin@urlinkpublishing.com

URLink Print and Media is committed to excellence in the publishing industry.

Book design copyright © 2019 by URLink Print and Media. All rights reserved.

Published in the United States of America

Library of Congress Control Number: 2019914510
ISBN 978-1-64367-828-3 (Paperback)
ISBN 978-1-64367-829-0 (Hardback)
ISBN 978-1-64367-827-6 (Digital)

16.09.19

Preface

On 01/31/2018 a medium and a recent acquaintance of mine whose voice I heard coming from behind me said...They're watching. I asked her "what are you talking about". She said "they are watching us and they don't want you to write the book". I told her "I don't give a #@x* what they want, I'm going to do what I damn well please". Since our acquaintance began we both realized we were being watched. Both of our homes have been broken into and some of our personal identification has been stolen. Their focus of interest at the time seems to have been the documents that identified us. One outer apparel item of mine was also taken along with the notes I jotted down on a remote view I was doing across the country on a Bigfoot incident. I found it more than interesting that the woman claiming to be a medium had previously worked at Nellis Air Force Base , a base where the "tall whites" are said to be there.

Recently I communicated with another person interested in Ufology that sent me a video on an abductee's experience which including his briefly speaking about the Tree of Life. Through the process of an occult initiation I have been inducted into what is called "the current". "The current" has put me into contact with beings who have the knowledge of the "Tree of Good and Evil". In my opinion, both good and evil need to be addressed. Since a scant few have mentioned the other side of the UFO coin, the evil one, I have found it more than necessary to bring it to the forefront. Not just anyone is capable of withstanding such extreme exposure to what so many may address as "paranormal events". My induction, through initiation into the occult has allowed me to bring what I perceive as their agenda forward.

Soon afterward I met a prominent woman in the ufology field. We discussed a particular alien race. Within that conversation I mentioned writing this book. I didn't mention what it was about, well, barely, finding what she said intriguing. In what appeared to be an out-of-the-blue statement she said, "I know what you're trying to do, people won't listen because they prefer to engage in fantasy. You're here to write this book; it's what you're supposed to do with your life".

I've arrived at the conclusions that I have because of what I have repeatedly experienced (having gotten the same results over and over again under "like" circumstances), combine it with science, my education, fact finding synchronicities, and the input from good and knowledgeable friends helping me sort truth from fiction on the path I have taken. In addition, I give many thanks to those who have gone before me culling information and, at times, having put themselves in harm's way. Their efforts have enabled their information to gravitate towards others bringing what was found to the forefront.

There are those today that are greatly influenced by theories that are built upon the basis of exact scientific experience. They cannot do otherwise than regard the contents of a book like this as a boundless absurdity.

CONTENTS

CHAPTER 1

A Messenger Comes

Until now I have been able to avoid bringing religion into the UFO phenomenon. I can no longer continue to do this despite the fact that heads turn away at the mention of the prospect.

Before I continue onward, I find it relevant to mention an unusual condition of my birth which was responded to by my mother's inhospitable, revile reflected in her actions taken towards me over the years.

What, and not necessarily who is the messenger spoken of that bears the caul? A caul/veil is a full-face mask. It is a type of a membrane that is found covering the face (or thereabouts) of a child at birth. These births consisted of both female and male children. They may come from any social or racial class, or any religious association without the limitation of a geographical boundary prescribed to them. The phenomenon may occur in as few as one in eight hundred thousand births. Because of this rarity, a special significance is attached to children born in this manner. I will only explain what are considered to be accurate descriptions of this phenomena and will put aside the many stories and myths which are often-times erroneous.

Caul births have a tendency to run in family <u>bloodlines.</u> Their births can be calculated in advance predicting the time and place of such. They often have peculiar abilities in many diverse ways not commonly found in the general population. They included "water witching" (finding underground water supplies), knowing changing weather patterns, and predicting when food supplies would become plentiful. Many of them are natural healers whereby they lay their hands upon people or they may be able to remote heal them from a distance. Many are considered to have great abilities in matters of judgment and, as such, in the ruling of nations because they have in their possession insight others find difficult to appreciate. Because of their broad range of disciplines that they have become known as "priests' which simply means "teacher".

The word "priest" came into being long before the religious notion of the word. In addition due to their exceptional insights, predictive nature of their births, and their leadership abilities, many cultures considered them to be "kings by right". Today, Buddhist groups still seek out those born with the veil/caul and bring them up accordingly to be their Dali Lamas. They are also seen as messengers sent by a higher force to guide mankind in those matters of physical affairs and in those of a higher spiritual nature. Throughout history those seeking power through might have attempted to destroy the "kings by right".

Their purpose is to serve mankind assisting them in understanding themselves, the world, and the universe within which we live. Their ability is based in reality; it is not contingent on belief therefore, it should be kept separate from religious dogmas.

The caul is called "The Veil of Tears" because baser types of people sense something very different about caulbearers. They will attack or even deliberately murder those that were their benefactor without realizing why they have done so. They are operating on a subconscious level hence, "the curse of the caul" was born. It was primarily the church of Rome that took action against them. They burned them as witches and heretics in the Middle Ages because it was believed that shedding their blood wouldn't be able to bring down a perpetrator's curse. Their deaths deprived both those that persecuted them and their communities within which they lived from the benefits that would come from following the natural way of things. Following the natural way of things is the Caulbearer's way.

They are called "natural" magicians and performed miracles at the request of the church. The church felt that caulbearers needed to be controlled especially after recognizing that those who took to the "cloth" pledging a life of sexual abstinence, still could not create the miracles they did.

It came to pass that these natural magicians were no longer murdered for their special feats but were trained directing their abilities thereby avoiding unintended, spontaneous acts that may have had undesirous outcomes. While those that continue to struggle attempting to attain positions of power through might still consider the caulbearer an outstanding issue to be dealt with. Caulbearers' continue to be seen as an object to be extinguished as is the knowledge and or the acknowledgment of them. Due to repeated attempts suppressing their persecution by those wishing to become kings by "might", the word caulbearer isn't found in standard dictionaries.

> Note: Any crown worn that has a closed top e.g. the
> Christ child, is a crown that signifies a birthright ruler.

Often times the caulbearer's parents perceived them as having issues adjusting to what their parent's perceived as a normal life. As a result of this, their parents often took them to a priest to have the rites of exorcism imposed upon them attempting to drive out the misunderstood influence. Their caregiver's-imposed trauma usually drove the children into a state of mental anguish.

Due to erroneous stories that have surrounded those born with the veil, they generally misunderstand themselves, what motivates them, and in what they sense. They've learned lessons through hard experience e.g. others avoiding them or acting in peculiar ways void of the bearers' understanding. Often times, to no avail, the bearer of the caul has attempted to find out why he or she feels the way they do. She or he may regularly perceive things that others cannot relate to declining to disclose what they are aware of for fear of ridicule, or being misunderstood. It is not uncommon to find a person born with a veil who becomes addicted to alcohol or other substances in a vain attempt to block out a world that fails to understand. Due to these circumstances, they have a high suicide risk. As a consequence, drugs are prescribed to them in a vain attempt to treat a misidentified diagnosis of a psychosis or a case of schizophrenia.

Their caul may have been destroyed at birth as it has been the policy of many maternity hospitals and, in particular, those run by religious groups. In some cases, a person may have been able to keep their caul or it may have been kept for them without their knowledge. This would have depended upon the degree of understanding of those attending their births; I was told mine was destroyed.

The worlds' main religions were based on the teachings of caulbearers. The names of well known figures that you may recognize born with a caul have been: Moses, Buddha, Joshua Ben Miriam, Marduk (ruler and king of Mesopotamia), Odin (also known as Wodin) all of whom were later worshipped as deities. There was also Dan (the first of the Seven Signs. He was known as the judge and the progenitor of the tribe of Dan), and Jacques De Molay, (the head of the Knights Templar who was burned alive).

Today those partaking in satanic/pedophiliac practices require their adult participants to have their children accessed and are assigned a value within the group. Since psychic ability is a gift passed through blood/genetics their blood is drunk hoping to attain the child's abilities.

In one of my many experiences, when I was in grade school on the occasions when we finished all of our classwork early, the nun/teacher would have special games for us to play; some of them were intuition games. The teacher thought I performed exceptionally well telling me this in front of my classmates and went on to say that she told the priests about me.

Shortly afterward I went to church during my lunch hour to pray and asked two of my friends to come with me. My friends and I went to church whereupon on this day I sat roughly four pews back from the confessional. The drape covering the priest's access to the confessional never touched the ground which allowed me to notice that the shoes of the man in the priest's confessional compartment weren't those of a priest. Tempting fate, I walked by the confessional further than an arm's length. In an aggressive

*attempt, I saw the man reach out to grab me. He had on
a suit jacket or a sports-coat. His clothing wasn't that of a
priests'. The three of us ran out of the church screaming.*

*My grandmother cared for me after school until my
mother could get off from work. While walking from school,
within one block of my grandmother's home, a car pulled
along beside me. The car had four men in it and all of them
were wearing "Kelly" hats and either wore a suit or a sport-
jacket. The man in the front passenger side did all he could
to lure me into his grasp. When I refused his last offer, I ran
screaming toward my grandmother's home with him in hot
pursuit. He chased me half of the block on the way to her
home before he returned to their vehicle which was likely
because I brought too much attention to their presence.*

Through the attachment of belief systems, the actual and true
realities of those that have been borne with the caul were adapted to
serve the dogmas of religious groups and cults throughout the world.

In the occult, some have what they perceive is a positive experience
however others do not. I talked to an occultist friend of mine that seems
to have what he perceives are pleasant experiences, experiences that
drive him deeper into the pursuit of this esoteric knowledge. Because
his life is turbulent, he sinks deeper into the occult trying to remedy his
life's situation. It is unknown if his life has naturally evolved that way
or that it has become that way as a result of his pursuit.

Those called saints have the ability to manipulate physical matter
which is another way of saying that they can perform a "miracle".
Because there are persons such as these, an interdimensional/
ultraterrestrial being is highly likely to show its true colors. The
interdimensional attempts to redirect their thoughts which affects
the original intent. Interdimensionals/ultraterrestrials often create a
series of dismaying circumstances and or events. These provoke a
series of emotions in those that are capable of producing a physical
change. Their thoughts are likely to be affected by their emotions
and through these staged events, he/she redirects their physical
change amending the natural course of things unwittingly toward an
outcome into the direction of the ultraterrestrial's agenda.

CHAPTER 2

First Sighting

I was married and in my early 20's. Despite struggling financially like so many young couples, our home never ceased to be filled with laughter. Because our marriage was so happy my husband's friends were a bit envious and, as a result, it prompted his younger brother to marry.

By this time my husband and I had been married approximately five or six years. It was a beautiful Summer evening. We stayed home a great deal but were getting cabin fever. We decided to take an evening drive. At that time, the city we lived in was relatively small. We drove to the outskirts of Fullerton, California before turning off of the main drag and were now driving on a less traveled road. I spied something off to my left and hurriedly told my husband to stop and pull over. I exclaimed, "what the heck is that"? His response was, "I donno". I noticed other cars were traveling past what we were looking at. None seemed to notice anything unusual. I presumed that this may have been because what we were observing was lit from its underside and its shape would have initially appeared to have been partially concealed to a vehicle traveling the allotted speed limit.

He made a U-turn which positioned our car so my side, the passenger side, was against the sidewalk. The two of us sat in the car watching a very large, flawlessly surfaced, silvery, saucer-shaped object hoovering two stories off of the ground. I remember thinking how aesthetic it was. It had no rivets or seams. It hovered over a grassy field surrounded by a chain-link fence. There was a multi-story building in the background not far away from it. This allowed me to determine that it was hoovering two stories off of the ground. Years before my father took me onto an aircraft carrier he served on. Having see it, it gave me perspective in estimating the size of this object. I knew that two large trucks could have easily driven around in it if it was nearly empty. My husband became even more worried when I wanted to roll down my window. He told me "no" and to keep the car's doors locked. We kept watching this thing while I glanced off and on at the car's clock on the dashboard for thirty minutes. I didn't see the grass move under the saucer-shaped object but I did see colored lights on the underside of the craft. I knew it had four colored lights however I could only see the red, blue, and green lights but suspected the fourth light was yellow because, in retrospect, I realized these colors represented "the four Cardinal Points".

Now that 30 minutes had nearly passed, I became frustrated. I wanted to see more than I had. I kicked the door open then proceeded to scale the chain-link fence. I barely took my second step onto it when my husband came from behind me and jerked me off of it by putting his hands into my back pockets before stuffing me into the car before speeding off. The next morning, I fixed breakfast and found him to be unusually quiet keeping his head down while he ate. I asked, "do you want to talk about it?". He said, "no and don't you ever bring it up again, I'll never talk about it". Our relationship was never the same all-the-while, as I watched, he became quieter and his personality and desires darkened. Within one weeks' time, after witnessing the event, he spoke of becoming fearful, worrying that he'd follow in his father's footsteps. He said how easy it would be to kill me and how he would do it. From then on, he became more strange and deviant.

I used to go out to dinner once per month as part of socializing our two girls. At those times I ordered a "to go order" taking it to work for my husband. He asked that I not bring him dinner anymore. He said he was being blamed for money missing from his work.

A car would park across the street nightly. It left its lights on; they pierced through our open-weave drapes blaring through them for hours while my husband was away night after night. At times, when he was supposed to have been home, more than once I found the backdoor unlocked and opened at 1:00 A.M. My husband was nowhere to be found; his car was gone. Oddities, maleficent, highly deviant, and dangerous issues continued. During this time, in the city where I lived, I witnessed an unusual occurrence. A <u>buzzard</u> circled our house for <u>seven</u> days. Having had a chance to reflect on it, I believe it was a sign. After discussing these issues with my parents, we all agreed the situation I was in was in was far too dangerous so I left to go live at their home with my two girls.

CHAPTER 3

Second Sighting

A good deal of time passed; I was the sole financial support for the three of us; it was really tough going. I only got three hours of sleep per day and felt as though I was being torn from both ends. My doctor told me I was expected to have died three times that year. As a consequence, my parents pressured me into marrying someone I didn't care for.

The two of us eventually purchased a new home in a recently built housing tract that was quite a distance away from where we both worked. Its location was more affordable than an identical, local home. It had plenty of room for the girls and a perfect backyard for them to have friends over; it was nearly the last unsold home available. I took over a deposit and plunked it down as soon as I could.

During this time, while I was still working and doing an outrageous commute, I decided to go to college attending Riverside City college. I did so well that my husband suggested that I quit my job. In my second year, along with some other classes, I took biological psychology.

The classroom door was opened and all of us were seated at the desks we chose. The instructor was six-foot-tall or so. He had white-blond hair, blue eyes, and looked like a powerhouse on two legs. I thought he could have easily picked up a man his size throwing him from the front of the classroom through the back wall without any perceived effort.

Our first class got underway and as he spoke my thoughts raced. I was enamored by what he relayed. I had so many questions; I tried to reserve them so as not to interrupt him but something odd happened. As he continued to lecture, walking in my opposite direction, I thought a question. He reeled around, walked up to my desk, looked me in the eyes, then answered that specific question. He continued once more walking into the direction he had been continuing his lecture as he once had. I had a second mental question which I asked and, like the first, he again reeled around, walked up to my desk, knelt in front of me, then answered my question. This continued for a bit. The class seemed to be in a state of shock and awe judging by the expressions on their faces. The back row tilted their chairs back leaning them against the wall in what seemed to be a subconscious effort to get away from a situation, a situation that they saw their instructor answer questions they never heard being addressed.

He talked about the human body, its abilities especially those regarding our senses, and some other biological things. Since I have heard what he had to say about the material he covered I haven't seen it disclosed in any text book nor have the doctors I've talked to heard of such things. His knowledge was truly engrossing.

> *According to a Lieutenant Colonel, some people are specifically taken/abducted for their psychic abilities' genetic material. He stated that this ability is being bred out of us (as evidenced in a study validating the lack of this ability in modern humans) which would make us less independent and more interdependent especially with artificial intelligence. I was able to talk to Charles James Hall on February 11, 2018, regarding my class instructor I mentioned above. Mr. Hall asked me, "was it a Grey you were talking to?" I said, "no it was a tall, white, instructor". Charles paused then looked at me intently. I then said, "Oh…oh.now I know what you mean, he altered his physical appearance to appear as I saw him".*
>
> *Further down I've written about the ability to be able to do this and how this may come about when I discuss the experiment I did on frequency.*

> *Charles went on to mention that the Nordics and Greys aren't telepathic but that they do have a device that allows them this function. I continued to talk to Charles regarding the experiment I ran. For those of you who don't know Charles.... he has written the Millennial Hospitality books, has served in the military, is a physicist, and has had interactions with "the Tall Whites" and with the "Greys" at the Indian Springs, Nevada base. The experiment I ran had to do with changing physical appearance which is why I understood what Charles meant when he asked me if I what I saw was really a Grey. I told him what I did in my experiment. He agreed if I truly did what I claimed in my experiment then it would have changed its shape.*

The more I telepathed with the instructor the more frequent and the more intense my headaches became. As a consequence, finding it unavoidable, I knew I had to withdraw from his class. I mentally thought, "I'm sick and I have to withdraw from your class". I was able to pick up his thought for the first time when he telepathed to me "that's okay". I was disappointed, he seemed too agreeable. I was learning so much: this was the last thing I wanted to hear. I surely didn't want to miss anything he had to say. This I also told to Charles in our conversation. Charles said that my having headaches in the instructor's presence indicated that I had a credible experience because the device they carry enabling them to telepath would have given me headaches.

After having withdrawn from his class, while in the process of walking to another one of my classes and within the confines of the building's quadrangle, I saw the instructor sitting on a cement bench across from me, I hid behind a pillar testing him to see if he could hear my thoughts. He immediately lifted his head in my direction. I thought that by this point there wasn't any need to hide; he knew exactly where I was. I picked up a strange and unexpected feeling from him. I felt that he was there because he had to be, exempting him from bliss. He was somehow out of his time. We continued to telepath each other for a brief moment. His thoughts were sarcastic.

Suddenly he gripped the underside of his bench then jettisoned off running toward me using his long strides. I'm a short person and I was no match for him but I gave it a go and we found ourselves both running through the crowds knocking and hitting people out of our way, hearing the students shouting at us as we cleared our paths.

I arrived at a three-tier staircase that led me down to where I parked. I was in the middle of the first tier when I stopped and turned among the milling students attempting to see how close I was to him. I saw him standing on a cement planter at the top of the staircase looking for me. I thought it odd that he didn't pick out a stationary object such as myself before I came to the realization that he didn't recognize me by sight, he recognized me by my thoughts. I left my mind blank while getting out to my car as soon as possible. Later I started to reflect exactly why he may really have been working there. Was he looking for something or someone among the hundreds of people he had exposure to on a weekly basis? Was he a Grey as Charles suspected? In the days that passed I kept my distance. Finally, I looked across the quadrangle into his classroom. I'd always see seated students but I never saw him. I was deliberately late to class one day to see if I could see him but I still couldn't despite positioning myself at different angles to get a better view. I thought if what Charles had said was true, and he was able to change his form, perhaps he was masking himself. Charles agreed.

After my last class for the day, I saw a non-credited class offered on a poster on a bulletin board. I thought it was out of the school's character to have a psychic teach on campus. At the time I've never seen a working psychic so I thought it would be interesting to attend. Now that we were all seated, she introduced herself and took the notes out of her pocket that she wrote about each individual seated at his or her desk. She didn't give ambiguous descriptions; she gave specific, individualized descriptions with 100% accuracy. They "wowed" all of us.

I found the class quite interesting. Nearing its end, we were asked to guess within her set perimeter, what she was thinking. Three of us including myself guessed correctly and, as a reward, we were given a free reading. I was the last to receive a reading. She took a deep look at me then proceeded to say "I am afraid for you (all-the-while stepping back) something is going to happen to you within the next day or two and I don't think you'll live". Thinking that this was way over the top, I said, "then why don't you tell me what it is so I can try to sidestep it?" She said, "I don't think you'll be able to, I can't help you". I thought, "just wonderful!" I went home and nothing happened. I felt grateful that I was 50% in the clear of the predicted event. The more time passed the more I was able to put aside the dreaded warning, thinking or rather hoping that it was all a bunch of hooey.

The following evening my children stayed with their father. Previously my husband made his decision to volunteer to work this same evening. What appeared to be an incredulous lighting storm arose. I've never been afraid of lightning but felt that this was a highly abnormal event. I called my husband imploring him to return home fearing for the worst. The lightning was like nothing I've experienced before. I told him that the lighting sounded like it was being generated from directly above our rooftop. I could hear the electricity vibrating in the walls electrifying them while they resonated the sound… zzzzzz zzzzzz zzzzzz. He refused to come home even after he heard the walls vibrate with electrical current over the phone. I hung the receiver up then went into the den while looking around for any physical changes that could plausibly be occurring other than the walls continuing to vibrate. I kept my distance from the walls and was afraid to touch almost everything.

Now that I've arrived in the den, I looked out of the window facing the front yard. Above me were partitioned beams allowing our atrium to get sunlight. I saw thick bolts of lightning jettisoned out in a radius from above the roof. I wanted to go outside to determine what the lighting's point of origin was but I was too intimidated after reflecting on the psychic's warning.

During the storm, or what I thought was a legitimate storm, I looked across the street and saw my neighbor's head resting on his windowsill while having his drapes partly partitioned. It was quite a sight just seeing a human head on a sill, visible then invisible while thick bolts of lightning tore through the sky. I finally realized that my neighbor was kneeling on his carpet. His drapes closed then, abruptly, his front door flashed open slamming against the side of his garage wall. He ran, as if for his life, across the street to my house; I was already making my way to the front door. He knocked feverously; I opened the door inviting him in. He declined my invitation but, in the process, he told me there was a lightning storm. With something so blatantly obvious I have to admit I was a bit sarcastic telling him I knew. He said "you just don't get it; it's above your house and it's nowhere else. It's right on top of your roof, it's not touching your roof but it's right above it" and, with that, he ran across the street just as he came, slamming his door closed, assuming his kneeling position, watching above my roof.

Now and then I'd see my neighbor coming home and would cordially say "hi". Upon hearing me he'd look over his shoulder at me, would quickly glance at my rooftop, then back at me, then back at my rooftop, then he'd rush into his home slamming his door quickly, drawing his drapes. This continued until he left within one week's time. I never saw a "for sale" sign on his home. He may have found it worth his while to abandon it as many have suggested. The question is: Did he see more than lightning above my roof?

The following evening my children were back home and I was studying in the den. I glanced to my right looking across the living room out into the yard through our open-weave drapes. Seeing a circle of light on the ground I was flabbergasted when I saw a man standing within it. My oldest daughter walked across the den's entry making her way toward her room. I stopped her by asking, "do you see anything out there?" She exclaimed, "mom, a man is out there watching us". I grabbed both children, shut out the lights. We went into a huddle in the kitchen where our view could be hidden. I worried that our images would reflect off of the surfaces of our appliances projecting them to the windows above us. It didn't take him long to figure out where we were. He stood looking through the window above the cupboards trying to see over them then he tried to gain entry through the glass door to my left where I previously placed a dowel in the door's track. He rattled the door up and down ferociously and from side to side trying to free it from its track.

Fortunately, there was a phone off to the side of the cupboard. I phoned the police. They arrived in a matter of minutes but found nothing.

Due to the electricity that accompanied the event, I believe a porthole opened up allowing all manner of things to come through into our domain. In the following, I thought I'd mention a few incidents and point out some ensuing negative events that I believe were the result of this activity.

I purchased an early American bedwarmer to use as a decorative item in my kitchen. It had a hole-punched design of a five-point star on its lid for its decoration. I hung the bedwarmer upside down on the kitchen wall thinking it was more aesthetically pleasing. Looking at it, with its point down, I thought it's just a design right? Nothing can come of this. It's a bedwarmer; hundreds of homes have had them but still, they probably weren't hung with their points down.

All of the homeowners in our housing tract had brand-new, strongly built, dog-eared wood fencing. As soon as I finished hanging the bedwarmer, I heard a dog barking two streets away. The Doberman ran through his gate busting it down then he ran around to the block in back of us, crashed through their front wood gate, ran through their backyard, blasted a hole through their back fence (which happened to be the same fence as our back fence), and charged at me. Having been outside at the time I barely slammed the glass door in time. After having done so he barked angrily, jumped up against the door a few times rattling it, then back he went the way he came.

I usually stayed up a while longer while the rest of the family went to sleep. Between work, school, and house chores, I still was only able to get three hours of sleep per day. Studying, I sat on the living room couch. For some reason I decided I'd test myself to see if I could do some of the psychic things I used to. I was still able to advance the hands on the clock and, since I was on a roll, I thought I'd try cracking the formal living-room dining tabletop. I concentrated for roughly 30 minutes then I heard a loud crack. I thought "wow, I did it"! I walked over to the table; it looked like it was in perfect shape but then again, the lighting wasn't that great at the time. I waited until the weekend when I was off work and had more light before I did a recheck. I saw that I split one of the legs from its table's top. I never tried anything like this before and I have to say I was pretty impressed.

Things started getting weird again. The next morning, we found an end-table that I was sitting by (the previous evening while using my psychic's ability) weighing over 50 pounds that had a heavy ceramic lamp on top of it in the middle of the hallway. It impeded our access to or in leaving all three rooms e.g. the living room, the girls' rooms, and our bedroom. The lamp had been unplugged or the cord had been taken out of the wall because it wasn't long enough to reach into the middle of the hallway. We moved the two items back in place but its impression endured through the many times I vacuumed. The end-table that was moved into the hallway may have been a metaphor of things to come. It may have represented a coming division among all of us.

The paranormal events persisted keeping us on edge like shaken cats in a box. My oldest daughter and I saw a house-sized cat made of what looked like blue light; it walked in-between us. It had brighter pinpoints of light that ran from its head, feet, then to its tail that were connected by lines of light that were dim. It looked as though we were looking at its nervous or chakra system or even an illustration of a drawn constellation. The blue-light cat sauntered by, turned the corner, then went into her bedroom. Later on, my eldest finally confessed, telling me she was scared. She said a cat would come out from under her bed, would jump onto it and it would turn into a panther-looking cat (all black). It had large glowing red eyes. I had a blessed cross over her door but it had no effect; perhaps it was because she didn't believe in it. (It is said that demon beings have glowing red eyes.) It would stare at her positioning itself on her bed so as to be between her and the door in her room bringing an end to any attempted exit. I told her to sleep with her sister in her sister's room. Now that she was in her sister's room, I could hear the two of them screaming while the bed violently hopped around with both of them on it as they hugged each other hanging on for dear life.

A Native American elder and ghost hunter has found that children rather than ghosts have affected a home to such a degree that it was thought that the home may have been haunted. Children don't have the mental blocks adults often do nor their non-belief thereby imposing restrictions upon themselves. In a chapter further down I will go on to explain mans' ability to create.

Six and ten-year old's have moved objects when they sleep and have been found floating in a room. Most of the time these events are magnetic interferences that can be and are caused by external forces but are not limited to e.g. iron ore under a house. The haunted houses he has investigated are found to have high magnetic interferences. He's acknowledged that we are "spiritual amplifiers" for ghosts, orbs, and etc. Stories and or events are a vibration/ frequency: they interact with our DNA. All communication reacts to our body's vibration and spirit.

On a side note, this is why English (with its 26 letters) is not considered one of the holy languages because it is vibration deficient. The translation of ancient language and our true understanding of it has to be a vibration that our DNA understands.

While cleaning out closets I found the doll in a box that I put away some time back. As I held the doll, I reflected on my history with it. I hoped that, perhaps, what had previously occurred may have been due to an overactive child's imagination. Taking the doll out of the box I showed it to my oldest daughter. She immediately fell in love with and wanted it. She chose to put it on her dresser as I had. Later she told me that at night she'd hear a noise coming from the doll on her dresser and when she got up in the morning, she said it faced the wall. She said the doll wouldn't look at her.

My father spent much of his youth at sea. When he came home he brought beautiful gifts for my mother and I. I was very appreciative to have been the lucky recipient of some pretty fantastic and unusual toys. One of these was an 18" tall Geisha doll. It was totally finished in silk including her face and hands. Her features were all painted by hand.

Her right arm was bent into the shape of an "L", bending at her elbow. Her right hand supported a Samurai Helmet, the type you may have seen with the horns on top. I believe that she represented the Goddess of War. As a child, I put all of my Japanese dolls on top of my dresser but reserved the center spot for this one. I'd wake in the morning and would find the doll facing the wall. Seeing this I made deliberate attempts to condition myself to wake up each night, hoping to find what was occurring. On one particular night, and, as I tested on others, I awoke hearing a rapid thumping noise at midnight. I saw the doll rocking and teetering as it vibrated around making its 180 degree turn until it faced the wall. Seeing this happen over and over again while nothing else in the room seemed to be affected including the many things I had on top of my dresser I felt afraid and put the doll away into a box. I too felt that the doll wouldn't look at me however, I couldn't part from it, it was such an exquisite gift from my father. Somehow, I was able to hang onto the doll despite life's tumultuous times.

As per usual a negative pattern of behaviors, relationship issues, and temperament changes ensued resulting from the plausible UFO activity that coincided with the presence of the anomalous being. We were filled with fear and dread at the onset of each new occurrence. As a result of these past and present activities my current and also my second husband started drinking to the point where it became disruptive.

I was so proud of my daughters and enjoyed hearing how wonderful others thought they were. Through our experiences with the recent phenomena their behaviors dramatically changed. My oldest was the most evident of the two and many times I couldn't believe what I came home to.

Our work commute took a toll on our cars and our purse so we decided to sell our home in an attempt to move closer while remaining in the suburbs if possible. A couple from back East purchased our home. He was a bit angry having to share equal ownership with his wife according to state law and having to purchase a car for her, a necessity to get around in our state.

While I packed, one of our immediate neighbors came over. I never told him what went on in our home. He knocked on our door, and, keeping his head down, he asked if he could talk to me for a minute. Sitting down at the kitchen table, mostly looking down, he proceeded to tell me that he only liked two of the homes that were left, the one he purchased and ours. He said he walked into ours first and stated that it just felt weird. I found this remarkable because two saleswomen that at one time came to our door said they could literally feel the house from over one block away. Far from a religious man, our neighbor looked at me saying, "did you ever notice that the shadow of the beams above the atrium and the front door form an upside-down cross on your walk when you enter the home and when you leave the cross is right-side up? Shortly after our conversation he listed his home for sale and was able to move before we were.

Our new neighbors, a young couple, were barely there for any time whatsoever before they moved too. They were in the house situated on the side of ours. She started to beautifully redecorate their home when, in the process, it became infested with huge flying cockroaches that were inches long, coming in through their drains. I could hear her tormented screams. She said the roaches were all over their ceilings and their walls. Then their earth started to form mounds that erupted with wasps and roaches where none seemed to have been before. This only happened in the vicinity of and next to our home where the strange lighting occurred. Shortly after hearing her story I had a horrible ant infestation. The neighbor to the other side of us hung a velvet painting near his front doorway of Satan. I caught him going outside with a rifle to shoot an owl, an odd sight for one of our residential neighborhoods. To this day I still have nightmares about that home and feel even more convinced that a porthole did open up. I believe we have mistakenly associated alien encounters as paranormal encounters in too many instances. What you have read here is very important because it leads to supporting the chapters on Resetting Human Frequency and especially in the chapter, God Rests in the Brain.

CHAPTER 4

Aiming for a Fresh Start

I n the interim, while we were looking for a new place to live, we began painting our picture of a fresh start having rented a very nicely appointed apartment with rolling landscape, streams, peaceful views, and desirable amenities. When we initially previewed our soon-to-be, temporary home. I felt very uncomfortable on the premises but, given how nicely appointed it was, I didn't give it much thought. I felt as though something was there and even looked up the fireplace flue to check. We were the first residents to live there despite this I still felt I had a reason for concern. It wasn't long before we completed our "fresh start" by adopting a very curious, intelligent, and playful calico kitten we named "Pepper".

While working, doing housework, the kids, and my schooling, I thought I'd look into the continued strange things that kept going on hoping to make sense out of what we've experienced. I had hoped that peace would come through understanding. My husband told me about a Unitarian Church that I may be interested in and, nearly simultaneously, I joined a secret mystery school to expand my search.

I started out by taking a class offered in the counselor's home who was affiliated with the church. The counselor kept a pet wolf that would go ballistic sensing my arrival before I could be seen from her home or from her block for that matter. One evening, through a guided meditation, we were taught how to enable our astral bodies to leave our physical bodies. When we were done, and finally returned to our physical bodies, the counselor remarked how amazed she was witnessing what she said my aura had done so incredulously.

It was customary for her to burn a white candle in her classes. She did it to burn off any negativity that may have been brought in by anyone. Because I was still seeking answers, we communicated with each other off and on by phone. Often times our conversations were disrupted by something that sounded like "white noise" over the telephone line which is often the case when paranormal activity occurs. She told me that the last time I was there and had gone home for the evening, the flame on the candle shot up to at least 1 foot tall and, as she watched, a language and symbols were being inscribed into it. I asked what the symbols and language were. She refused to tell me; perhaps she didn't know herself. I haven't stopped wondering about it. Needless to say, she discarded the candle.

Having joined the secret mystery school, I took their correspondence course. Some of the schools promise enlightenment but they never mention which light you will be coming upon. At the time I thought it would be something good as many do. The name Lucifer means light bearer. I found my correspondence coursework both uninteresting and monotonous; none-the-less, I moved along with it. Their instruction came in the form of pamphlets. The new pamphlet I recently received required that I perform a ritual.

Now that it was late, and our home was settling down for the evening, the family was either in bed or nearing their bedtimes. I thought this was a perfect opportunity to apply myself to the new task set before me. The apartment, being new, had fresh seals on the doors and windows, the flue was shut on the fireplace, and it was draft free and secure.

I added a couple of things outside of what was required to the ritual that I would be performing. One was a white candle and the other was a double terminated crystal with an elaborate silver band in its center enveloping a cabochon garnet.

The ritual started out quietly enough but evolved into something I hadn't anticipated. The candle's flame shot up, then the flame laid onto its side projecting at least one foot out, pointing at me as if I was magnetic North, then, wherever I moved, the flame would follow me and continued to point toward me. Moving back into my original position, wearing my satin, flannel-backed, heavy nightgown, a wind came into the room blowing the gown causing it to flap against the couch so forcefully that the gown showed my form. I heard a noise that increased in volume coming from a corner in our living room. It became so loud that it sounded as if I had my head in a beehive. This buzzing sound has been reported in out-of-body experiences, abduction and near-death experiences, and with the phenomenon of entity encounters that are created in an interdimensional shift. After I completed the ritual I was required to submit a report. When submitting my report, I took the opportunity to ask the school what it was that made the sound I heard. They wrote back stating that it was the sound of the universe.

The following is an account of a beehive sound:

In the story of "Our Lady of Fatima," a group of mediums received a message using automatic writing. Automatic writing is a technique used by an occultist to contact entities. The procedure is generally frowned upon because the contactees are often fallen angels or demons that are said to habitually lie. The mediums' writing was published in several papers. It stated that something wondrous would happen in Portugal on May, 13th. The entity that was channeled through the medium identified itself as "the Bright Morning Star" which happens to be a synonym for Lucifer.

On the day before May 13th, when the Fatima apparition appeared to the three children, another entity appeared to a shepherd boy telling the boy not to be afraid.

Over 100 years ago from the Fatima Moors in Portugal, three illiterate children had an encounter with a being that communicated with them telepathically. According to the original handwritten documents, the children never said that they saw Mary; they said they saw an entity that came from the sky.

When the entity appeared to the children the people heard a buzzing noise reminiscent of being in or near a <u>beehive</u>. *This same sound has been frequently reported in UFO encounters. All three children saw this entity but only the females could hear it. The entity offered them something to eat and drink however Francisco declined the drink that was offered to him. As it turned out there was also a fourth witness that had an encounter with a being in the exact spot that the apparitions took place with the three children. Carolina Carrera was the fourth witness. She was twelve years old at the time when she had her encounter. She gave her testimony to the parish priest, Father Fierra. Her account went unnoticed for decades. In her account, Carolina said she met a blond-haired figure while tending her sheep; blond hair is unlike the hair seen on the Portuguese people. Caroline couldn't tell the gender of the blond haired being because of the length of its hair. Carolina turned to look at her sheep and when she looked back, the blond-haired figure was gone. She looked around for it and found, to her amazement, that it stood above the tree it initially appeared by; it was hovering in midair. This is the original story however, is likely to have been obfuscated/managed by the church's authorities. Having androgynous beings floating above the tops of trees is hardly normal. Something supernatural was going on in Fatima that had nothing to do with what was on the official record their people had been conditioned into accepting as "truth".*

Having heard the rumors of a rendezvous, the people anticipated they would experience a holy phenomenon so they assembled on the site. The three little shepherds arrived thirty minutes earlier than expected. The girls were crowned with flowers and were carried to their meeting place. On this, a balmy day, Lucia asked the crowd to close their umbrellas. The visible sign was announced beforehand and it was ready to be produced. An immense multitude gathered that could be seen from the road. They turned toward the sun; the sky was now free of clouds. The sun (UFO) spun about itself like a ring of fireworks. The crowd saw this as a sign from heaven. They wailed, screamed, and cried out hysterically. These are hardly the reactions associated with something that brings comfort and security as would a loving and a forgiving God. Having been made void of utilizing critical thinking, testing, or questioning after witnessing an event such as this, they readjusted their thoughts arriving at a false conclusion that what they saw was the sun thereby they reassured themselves of their faiths' righteousness having previously been conditioned not to question and instead to accept on faith.

Often times what are called "sun-miracles" show a pulsing orb and, in some cases, it appears as though the sun is actually advancing downward toward people. These apparitions appear as amorphous blobs of light. It is impossible to tell what they are yet many assume what they are having chosen optimism over reality. "Fatima 2, Strange Phenomenon" revealed a never-before-seen photograph of an object in the sky that could only be described as a disc. The photo was taken from the original glass-plates at the 'sanctuary' in Fatima. The photograph was discovered by Jose Machado.

The following statements may be considered warnings. The Apostle Paul said that Satan would come with all of the signs displaying wonders to deceive. What happened in Fatima was a harbinger of deception. Jesus warned that even the elect would be deceived. Both Jesus and Paul expected us to have encounters with the dark side (peternormal). Unfortunately, we're conditioned at an early age by our religious instructors to have a faith-based religion as opposed to one that allows us to discern what is from God and what is not. Accepting things entirely on faith arrests us from this discernment. However through our conditioning, by choosing fact over faith we find ourselves ridden with guilt having strayed from our "as instructed" faith-based system.

Now that I've finished the ritual, I started putting my tools away. I recoiled with a jerk seeing that the crystal glowed a brilliant red. It appeared to have a self-contained light within it. The bright light indicated that the crystal's frequency had deviated. I know this all sounds so very strange until the reason why has been understood then internalized. It is because of this that I've provided the following explanation below:

> *Electrons were trapped in the vibration (sound waves) of the beehive-sound I heard that were in their process of moving from where they were into a solid (the crystal). When the sound moves (vibrates) it transports electrons and their signals into a solid from moving them from one place to another e.g. like those pixels in a CCD camera that are transported to a readout device. In my particular experience, they were transferred from the beehive sound into the crystal and perhaps myself as well. Like miners that have trapped gold nuggets into their sluice box, electrons can be put into a solid making a device easier to fabricate e.g. the transportation of an energy/entity or an indescribable being into another container such as the crystal which has turned the vibrations into strong electrical fields. This creates an electrical pressure (for the lack of a better word) which is a type of download process.*
>
> *The vibration had different energies existing within it. How it affects or pushes the electron into another orbit would have changed the crystal's color. The change corresponds to the visible region of the electromagnetic spectrum.*

In retrospect, after I performed what I thought was a ritual, I have come to the realization that it was much more than that…it was an initiation. Years later I found what its purpose was, it was to connect a person to the current. To best describe, it's as if one is a lightbulb with a wire connecting that bulb to the next bulb, the same wire carries the same electricity to all of these bulbs off of the same wire as far as the eye can see; they all become as if they are one and are able to communicate with each other through the same current that is carried through all of them. Simply put, they hear our thoughts and those that have been initiated can hear theirs. I'd like to point out what I hypothesize on Egyptian art/hieroglyphs regarding the frontal eye. It is painted or inscribed onto their figures. It represents those that have been initiated. It also alludes to the R-complex. You will see that not all are depicted with the eye drawn this way.

> *Supposedly the highest-ranking Druid in North America, a 33-degree Mason and Mormon bishop said that if you want to understand the Luciferian mysteries you had to join a Masonic lodge. The initiate is told that when he comes into the lodge the initiate is prayed for but when he receives his 3rd degree (an initiation similar to a witch's initiation) the initiate is asked to pray for himself because in the journey he has embarked upon many men have lost their lives in the process or have nearly done so. The initiate treads on a path toward enlightenment but it is never said where the light comes from. At the time he didn't consider that it was the "light" of Lucifer, the Light Bearer.*
>
> *Having gone through the York's Rite, and being a member of the Knights Templar, which is part of the commandry, he received an invitation to join the Ancient Illuminated Seekers of Bavaria. He went through the first initiation into the Illuminati which is called the Luciferin Initiation. Part of what he learned there in the underbelly of Freemasonry involved an incredible amount of wicked sexual practices which included child abuse. The initiate went on to say that the men involved in this believed that they could live forever on the sexual innocence of children by stealing their life's force energy, the Spark. They chose this route to achieve immortality rather than the more difficult path which is being obedient to the almighty.*

Considering how well I was doing in school I took my husband's suggestion, quitting my job in order to go to school fulltime. It seemed like writing papers, doing outside research, and the time spent requiring volunteer work were endless. A sixteen through an eighteen-hour day were commonplace.

CHAPTER 5

Initiation Fallout

Since the initiation, my life as I once knew it had changed; there was no going back. Because of the plethora of things that have happened, I'm only going to mention some that dramatically impacted me throughout my life.

I was in the process of writing another paper. The dining room seemed a little dim even when the chandelier above my head was switched on all-the-while all of our other rooms seemed to be getting darker and much colder. It was 72 degrees in the house none-the-less I could see my breath before me as I expelled it.

I was writing another paper for one of my classes and could have used a little extra help; I wished I had a Thesaurus. Overhead, I saw that the chandelier starting to rock, swinging from side to side, casting its shadow across my paper while everything else in the room remained static. My vocabulary inquiries were answered; all I had to do was to think about needing an alternate word and it popped into my head. I didn't know what the words meant. I looked them up and they were always appropriate. During this time all knowledge seemed to have been made available to me; all I had to do was ask. Through this process I developed a voluminous vocabulary. The chandelier would swing regularly when I worked at the table. Whatever the presence was it made me aware it was waiting to assist me and, at the time I was grateful, thinking that I had been blessed.

During the time of my first shadow sighting, I looked toward my right, saw the carpet depress, felt the vibration of running on the floor, then I saw <u>three</u> shadow beings that ran from my left toward my right. They were different heights, slightly slouched, appeared as shadows, and the shadows were cast onto the wall as they ran past me.

> *"The Great Work" is part of the Amalantrah working. It is part of what Crowley thought was the intentional cultivation of spiritual growth. "The Great Work" involved contact with non-human intelligences or what are also called extraterrestrials.*

Lam Lore: According to O.T.O. chief <u>Kenneth Grant</u>:

- Lam is known to be a link between the star systems of Sirius and Andromeda.

- Lam is the gateway to the Void. Its number, 71, is that of "No Thing", an apparition.

- Lam, as a Great Old One, whose archetype is recognizable in accounts of <u>UFO occupants</u>.

- Lam has been invoked to fulfill the work set afoot by Aiwass; as a reflex of Aiwass.

- Lam as the transmitter to AL of the vibrations of <u>LA</u> via <u>MA</u>, the key to the Aeon of Maat.

- Lam is the occult energy beaming the <u>vibrations of Maat</u> and may proceed from that future aeon.

> *Crowley called himself "The Great Beast" and was once called "the wickedest man in the world". He also laid claim to being of "royal blood" (alien) and again this is another reference to bloodline. Crowley was a practitioner and an author in the realm of ceremonial magick and*

the occult inspiring countless followers to pursue the study of the higher mysteries and the esoteric.

Crowley's former residence, Boleskine House has been burnt down. It is alleged to be haunted or cursed because it was reportedly used for Satanist rituals and black magick ceremonies between 1899 and 1913. Crowley owned the property until 1913, after which it was owned by Major Edward Grant who committed suicide in Crowley's former bedroom with a shotgun. Following Grant's death, the legendary Led Zeppelin guitarist, Jimmy Page, purchased the property. Page collected Crowley's relics and writings and believed the site's dark history would inspire his songwriting. While he lived at the property Page reported paranormal experiences and terrifying encounters with what he described as "pure evil". For unknown reasons, Page unceremoniously sold the property in 1992. Since then the house has changed hands several times between private owners.

According to the Thelemic legend, in 1918 by Crowley's own admission, the purpose of the Amalantrah invocations were to open an interdimensional portal that would allow access to beings from other dimensions. One of the beings that came through this portal, the one Crowley sketched, was named Lam (an entity class). "The depiction bore a startling resemblance to the popular conception of a Gray depicted on the cover of Whitley Strieber's "Communion". The working also allowed other alien Grays passage onto Earth's plane. This portal may have been enlarged further by Parsons (a jet propulsion laboratory founder and rocket fuel scientist), and by Hubbard the Scientology and Dianetics founder in 1946 with the commencement of the Babylon Working. The working was based on ceremonial sex magick and allowed for a shift in human consciousness. _This magick is likely used by MK Ultra_ and those using children in their occult sexual practices. I hope you're starting to see a pattern whereupon human consciousness is being directed and that there are multiple ways of opening a porthole. Your "**Spark**" is being used to create a condition or a thing.

Concurrently there is a manuscript, the title of which I won't disclose, is circulating among specific members in a particular organization. Those members wish to "regularize the mode of rapport and intend to construct a magickal formula establishing communication with Lam. Invoking Lam entities through magickal portals intentionally creates rifts in time and space which brings them into physical manifestation here on earth.

Michael Bertiaux is a Lam invoker and contactee. In his view, Lam is the "subterranean burgeoning of Lucifer-Gnosis (intuitive knowing). This would mean that to know Lam is to know a welling-up from the unconscious of an inner knowing of Lucifer. It is important to bear in mind that occultists may not necessarily see Lucifer as the devil, but rather as the "light bringer" who fell to earth.) He felt contact with Lucifer-Gnosis, the Grey, is the appropriate path toward human spiritual growth that Crowley called "The Great Work". Using the language of Crowley's time, certain non-human intelligences such as Lam are what we today would term "extraterrestrial."

I had an eight carat, trillion cut, amethyst stone set into a ring with a diamond. The Amethyst was enveloped by gold leaves. In the amethyst's lore, it is said to be the stone of kings because it was used by them to detect their enemies. When the king's enemies were near the stone turned colorless. Curious to see if this was a myth, given my circumstances, I went to my jewelry box visually scanning it and wondered where my ring was. Even though I saw it I looked right past it, not recognizing it at first because the stone had turned crystal clear. The Amethyst was one of my favorite pieces of jewelery. The ring eventually regained its color and, when it did, I put it on and went to school. I arrived at the elevator and held its door open for a paraplegic or he may have been a quadriplegic seated in his wheelchair. He looked calm until he glanced up and saw my ring. His facial expression changed from placid to terror. Shaken, he looked at the ring, then at me, then back at the ring. Hurriedly he backed up and wouldn't board, instead, he waited for the next car.

Sometime later the ring was stolen due to my due diligence. I was told that the thief knew the power the ring possessed which is why it had been taken. The person disclosing this also said that the ring could also be disarmed and she, the person who stole it, should have realized that when she took it. By now the mutable odor of cat urine could be smelled at different locations in our home. The scent was usually by our closet or restroom, an intersecting point, a point where the paranormal and physical worlds cross each other. This intersection is called the veil. This symbol of the cross was used long before Christianity came on the scene and it is a representation where the two worlds intersect with one another.

I was washing my hair in the shower and had soap suds streaming down my face. Through my closed eyelids I saw a bright light. At first, I thought my husband was playing around with a flashlight. I was finally able to clear the soap from my eyes and saw a bright white orb about two feet in front of my face. I said "hello" and away it flew around the shower curtain opening and out of the bathroom.

After the little white orb came visiting, I awoke in the morning partly remembering what I thought was a very bad dream. I dreamt three very repugnant looking women violently locked me into what looked like a brown box. I'm not cooperative in the least when it comes to doing things against my will. None of us were clothed. I remember a black symbol being put onto the box. Once dredging through my magickal diaries I reflected on the symbol that I kept at the time. I noticed that it was a stylized, very unique, black colored sperm. It would have had to have been a very specific one. The drawing may provide clues suggesting a plausible genetic intercession/ manipulation. Unlike my drawing at the time, the sperm was symmetrical on both sides and it did have the rounded top.

Still in what I perceived was a dream state, after I was taken out of the box, a perfectly round orange dot was placed on a vertebra near the bottom of my neck. While continuing to have this dream a gigantic spider, larger than I was, bit me in the center of my left palm; it started to bleed. When you have one of these seemingly outrageous dreams you know how it is, you awaken and your heart and breathing are rapid then we ask ourselves, well thank God that didn't happen... it's a dream, right?

Upon awakening, I noticed that my left hand had been draped over the side of the bed with my palm up. I started to roll to my left to sit up to get out of bed but before I could finish, I saw that my palm was filled with blood. I was feeling anxious about the whole thing and woke my husband. I started to slide out of bed to empty the blood from my palm before it spilled onto the carpet when he said, "wait a minute, stop; you have something on your neck". "You have an orange dot on the back of your neck, let me try to get it off". I yelped a few times before he was able to eventually remove it. He scraped it so hard I thought my skin was going to tear off along with it. He couldn't figure out what it was made of. He said it wasn't wax. We tried finding it in the sheets but we never did and as for the blood, I had no wounds nor did anyone else. We didn't find a trace of blood anywhere in the home. There were no puncture wounds or scratches on anyone either. Years later, talking to a chiropractor, I inquired about the vertebrae's location. He said that the vertebra I spoke of was affiliated with the heart. I do have a heart issue so if I was given more of life's' time through this experience thereby extending my own life then this action reflects what I have spoken about previously regarding their having to give something in order to take something. This makes it appear as though there has been a (slight-of-hand) cooperation between the perpetrator and their host.

> *In the year 2017, at a symposium, I was told by a psychic that I had a son, a Grey. I didn't like her condescending expression that seemed to express "oh it's you". I felt that this reaction wasn't from her but instead it was from my alleged son, the Grey.*

Later on, I channeled some words. I was called a synonym for light, "Lucia" as well as "Delilah" and heard the word "dalliance" as well as "ménage a trois" and some other French word that I can't spell. Keeping the hours that I was I needed to take a nap. I awoke but was immobilized and felt myself being touched. Tried as I might I could not move. In the end, I had bruises in the shape of handprints on my inner thighs. The thumbprints were on the inner side of my legs making it impossible for me to have made them.

> *The Memphis Mitzrayim in Egyptian Freemasonry is one of the darkest things taught by a famous nineteenth century sorcerer wherein the initiate learns to develop the Congress of Devils whereupon the initiate learns to cultivate sexual relationships with fallen angelic beings. Typically, once having sex with one of these, he or she may believe that they will become angelic (a god or a goddess) because they may also believe that they have*

become as one flesh with the fallen celestial being. Please note that the gods and or goddesses of old were seen as angelic and or as fallen celestial beings.

Off and on I'd smell <u>smoke</u> coming from a mutable but specific area. (Since then I've learned that smoke is an indication of something thought of as demonic.) Along with everything else that was going on, we became aware of another presence that made itself known. I finally located its essence and had my husband come over while I tutored him regarding how to locate and feel it with his hands so he could describe what it looked like. My husband was five foot eight inches tall. The spirit was a male that was quite slim but taller than he was. We determined that he was wearing a sports jacket. Knowing that all was not going well, I put a double terminated crystal in the bathroom on a shelf. Some days later I noticed that it had turned much darker and looked as though it had charcoal on it. I knew it couldn't have gotten dirty. I took it out into the light and saw that it had clearly captured the image of a man wearing a sports jacket.

My oldest daughter came to me saying that she watched a doorway open up in the shared bedroom with her sister. A vivid green and bright, clean light would trace their closet door frame from left to right and people would go in and out of it. When the last being had gone through it the doorway would close from right to left. This usually occurred around 9:00 P.M. She said they would always watch it but were afraid to move when it occurred. I witnessed it once in their room and felt powerless to protect my children.

Shortly afterward I walked toward our bed that my husband was sitting up in watching TV. I had a vision and saw my body being carried along a dirt path followed by mourners through a grove of olive trees. My body was put into the side of a mountain that already had what looked like a cave dug into its side with a flat floor. Shortly after my burial the mountain's nose blew off and fell into the ocean. During this vision, without my saying anything, my husband turned his head toward me and said that I smelled strongly of olives. I wondered if the knowledge of this past life wasn't part of the knowledge that was being imparted to me from these beings.

What I was made to remember is probably why, as a child, I've always had an affinity for the area around Greece. Years later I described this same vision I had to a friend who was a member in my temple. He asked me if I was able to draw the coastline of what I saw. He had been to the area in the military and could also read Greek. He said what I drew was the coastline of Santorini. Now that the vision had passed my husband and I were sitting in bed by the TV when a red doorway opened up just like the green doorway did in my girl's room. Stunned, neither of us moved; really, what could we do but watch?

> *Years later, after writing my first book, I drove roughly 150 miles to the next town and, in the process, queried the desk clerk at the book store. She hadn't read my book but took me by my sleeve and said she had something to tell me ushering me to the back of the store. She told me that around 9:00 P.M. she would see a bright, green doorway open up from left to right on her property. The green light would trace her shed's door-frame and beings would go in and out of the illuminated doorway. When they were done the doorway would close from left to right.*

While fixing dinner in the kitchen I watched my cat walking before she sat in front of the doorway to our bedroom. The girls came next once observing the cat. Seeing this, my husband walked over and did the same. He called out to me saying "you have to see this". I walked over and briefly caught a glimpse of a blue orb taking the entire width of our queen-sized bed while it hovered above it. Nearly as soon as I arrived it blinked out.

My oldest and I were conversing, looking out into the living room. She said that there was a woman in a long, flowing, blue dress with long brown hair just below her shoulders in the glass of the curio cabinet. She asked, "mom, is that you"? I told her "how can that be, I'm right here beside you". She insisted "no, that's you". I'd like to point out that both the orb and the woman's dress were blue. In my first book, I wrote about multiple intersecting worlds; I'm assuming that this may have been an example.

The mathematics and astronomy professor, Bernard Carr, studied under Stephen Hawking at the Queen Mary University in London. "He believes that paranormal activity is real and is happening in another dimension." Professor Carr also believes that there's a hierarchical structure to the dimensions; many of which we cannot perceive. Periodically human consciousness is able to become aware, perceiving events occurring on other planes of existence that we are otherwise usually unable to interpret. His theory assumes that, if these events are taking place, they probably aren't happening in one of the three dimensions that we're capable of perceiving. For example…if a person existing in the third-dimension places an object in the second-dimension of space, it would appear to suddenly materialize to anyone within that dimension. Thus, Carr suggested what may seem like weird, impossible events could be easily explained if we take into account the fact that our brains are limited by the plain of existence that we're accustomed to interacting and operating in.

Perhaps my daughter was right, perhaps I was the woman in the blue dress coming into this dimension to rescue my family from overreach. I'll attempt to explain.

Howard Wiseman (Griffith University in Australia) led a team who believed that a quantum theory allowed for multiple versions of our universe to exist, overlap, and interact with one another. This suggests that we exist on another level/dimension. Reflecting on this statement I recalled the biblical phrase, "my Father's house has many mansions".

I started attending Sunday services held at a Unitarian church that was recommended to me by my husband via a fellow employee at his work. When I walked over to my car after the services were over I thought it was a little strange that I received an impression that at least <u>three</u> people had been trying to look into my car's windows to see what they could. Despite this, I kept attending and enjoyed the socializing but felt ill at ease wondering why, at the onset of service, that the children were always separated from their parents, taken into the back room, and were schooled separately. Apparently I didn't have the level of trust the others had. I later found out that they, at times, asked the children about their parents and what they did. None-the-less I was on a mission and was there to learn.

The lecture was very different this time. Speaking his first few words, the pastor looked at his listeners then he raised his head toward the back of the room appearing to be looking miles away as he recounted a recent event. Looking deeply into what appeared to be space, he told of his taking a drive out into the desert. He said he saw a "saucer" in the rocks and thought it had crashed. He parked his car nearby and walked to the pile of large rocks where the ship seemed to have been imbedded; "crashed" were his words. He said he saw <u>three</u>, short grey beings, all had large black eyes and were thin limbed. He didn't remember anything that may have transpired but could only recall feeling dazed afterward before getting into his car and driving off. He couldn't even remember how he finally arrived home; he only knew that he got there.

When he was done speaking, he shook his head a bit before mentally arriving back into the present. As was customary, after hearing a sermon or a story, we would go up and shake his hand and that of each other. It was time to greet each other with the pastor being the first. When it was my turn, he continued to hold onto my hand firmly, he cracked a maniacal grin on his face while still firmly gripping my hand then, the whole of his eyes turned completely jet black (black eyes are reported of the Djinn and of the Greys). He wouldn't let go of my hand. I'm not the fainting type but felt sickened, weak, and nearly went down before he finally let go. He nodded his head then I was immediately grabbed from behind by a woman and a couple of others. They pinned me against a wall while the pastor ran his hands about 4" off my spine, running them up and down it. I never returned to that church again.

In another instance, I was sitting up in bed looking at the ole tele when my husband strolled into the room. He stopped, his mouth gaped open, then he fell back against our mirrored closet doors. He managed to recover, stood up straight then didn't move for a while as he continued to stare at me. I tried to talk to him asking, "what is the matter"? He still didn't respond. I became worried because he looked like he was going to take an aggressive action toward me.

> *What had occurred is incredibly dangerous to an unwilling person taking on the form of an intervening spirit entering his or her auric field broadcasting the image the spirit has chosen to display. Those that the spirit has entered, their hosts, are not recognized and apparently are not heard by others. I've often wondered if this isn't the phenomenon of the shapeshifter. Some have been shot while having assumed another form and when their dead, dropped body has been found, they appear to be a human once again.*

He finally snapped out of it and told me that he saw a Native American male sitting up in our bed that had a single feather on top of his head. Later I found out that the single feather meant "messenger".

> *Having picked up my two girls after work we stopped at the grocery store on our way home. The three of them, husband and the girls, were waiting off to my right while I cashed out. Standing there I can remember feeling incredibly old. I could feel facial wrinkles and my wearing glasses. I could hear my kids say "where is mom?" the husband said, "I donno...she was right there". They all looked bewildered while proceeding to go out of the store looking for me. I called out to them but they couldn't hear me even as close as I was. I looked into a shiny object nearby and saw that I appeared to be an old woman. When I finally caught up with them, I asked why didn't you answer when I spoke to you. They said we couldn't hear you and when we looked where you were, we saw an old woman standing there.*

Most of the people that initially said they could help me through these trials didn't have the fortitude once their fear gripped them. Desperate, I went to a metaphysical store and purchased a reversal candle. The candle was half black and the other half was red. When it burned, I was instructed to see to it that the area was to become and remain peaceful and the user was to pray for the seven days that it took for the candle to completely burn down. Years later I found that the clerk gave me the wrong instructions.

I felt peculiar, awoke, and saw that I was being lifted up evenly off of the bed. Bending under the tucked-in blankets my toes ached. I took my right hand and tried to both slap and grab my husband's arm while gripping the blankets with my left hand trying to stay down. I called his name out several times before yelling at him telling him to look at what was happening. Things were getting rough; I quickly gave up trying to wake him and used both hands in my attempt to resist my levitation off of the mattress.

> *I listened to a Native American speak and by this time he was an elder. He had been groomed for his position since he was a child. In his teachings, he explained that our bodies and our spiritual system run on electricity. It is the same electricity/<u>current</u> that governs the universe. He stated things that go bump in the night are <u>sometimes</u> an amplification/echoes in our spirit/genealogy. What we feel is imagination really isn't, instead, it's an echo of what we've experienced in our past lives. He continued to say we give off strong magnetic fields which have already been proven to move an object and can affect the movement of wind.*
>
> *A friend of mine noticed that whenever a fire burned the flame/smoke would point toward me and would follow me in whatever area that I walked and its flames would even lean into the wind rather than retreat from it. Having acknowledged this, he had an astonished expression on his face. Continuing to wear the same facial expression he said, "wherever you move so does the flame and smoke...do you know it's following you?"*
>
> *An inventor named John Hutchison from British Columbia, Canada, in the 1990's, experimented with radio frequencies and electromagnetics. On a video he was able to capture the ability to levitate a 70-pound ball, wood, tools, and other materials teleporting them around*

his lab. He was also able to jellify metals (loosening their molecules). Because the military took him seriously, their scientists raided his home in March of 2002 at gunpoint using the Canadian police and joint task force agents to seize his lab equipment and his documents. It is no wonder that we are unaware of so much technology. It is being apprehended or managed while diversions like the media's theatrics, entertainment, and social disruption are designed to fill our spare time.

Now that another long dragged out day of drama had passed it was time to rest up for the unpredictable; as usual, I was the last one to bed. Once falling asleep I felt as if this was a "back-in-the-day" experience. I remember how comforting the bedding was and getting a deep totally refreshing, and peaceful sleep before all of this broke loose however, this time I felt enveloped in a "Christ presence". I felt love and protection; the timing of which couldn't have been more perfect. I had no pain nor fatigue in my body whatsoever. Wishing this pleasure would never end I'm sure I lay there with a smile on my face when suddenly my husband began trying to wake me, ferociously shaking and yelling at me to get up. It took me a while to awaken as if I was under some kind of a spell. When I finally awoke, he kept chattering that there was a white, cumulous-looking cloud floating one foot thru one and one-half feet above my body. It covered my entire length and width. I wasn't worried, telling him it was protecting me but unfortunately for me the cloud dispersed upon my waking and the comfort the cloud brought was gone.

The reversal candle finished burning and extinguished itself sometime during the night. After it had, I heard a vibrating noise (1:41 A.M., 05/11/1998) but couldn't manage to open my eyes. I wanted to but couldn't. After some delay, I was finally able to get up but only after the sound stopped. The noise came from my desk near our bed where the candle was originally placed into a large, silver-dipped, square, glass tray. The candle called attention to itself vibrating and skittering around the desktop while everything else remained static.

The apartment was the darkest it had ever been and it became difficult to make out the candle's' fine details in the impression that it left behind that I discovered later. I called the counselor I had been dealing with and told her what transpired. She told me to examine what remained of the wax in the tray. Shocked... I saw the image of a Reptilian in it. It was as clear as if someone pressed a signet ring into impressionable wax. Upon hearing the finding, her voice flooded with fear while telling me to immediately toss the wax into a dumpster outside of our home.

We didn't own a camera at the time. Here is what had been pressed into the red wax. I drew to the best of my ability at the time.

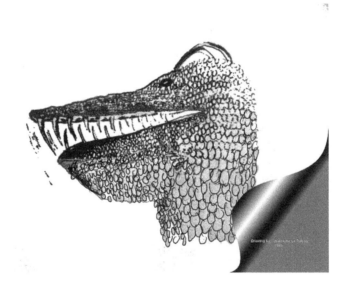

Drawing by: Antoinette Le Tutour

My husband's behavior continued to worsen and the evidence he left behind indicated a dalliance. I had two miniature clocks from Germany on the wall and knew our relationship was over when the owl clocked stopped working for no apparent reason on the sixth month, on the sixth day, and on the sixth hour (666).

CHAPTER 6

From Orbs to Greys

Sooner than expected, we finally received the news that we qualified for a condo in an area that we liked. We all moved in and got the kids settled into their new school. After some time had elapsed, I decorated our new place making it feel like a welcoming, comfortable home. By now the kids were home from school and sat with their step-dad watching T.V. while I cooked dinner. Suddenly three softball-sized, white orbs zoomed in through the fluorescent fixture above me, raced down the hall, then turned right, into our bedroom. I asked, "did you guys see that"? My husband said he saw it but the kids had been focused on their TV show. I took a break from what I was doing and went into our bedroom saying: "hi whoever you are". I received no indication of a response.

We had a very large, oak framed, three partitioned, beveled mirror above the couch. Unlike at any other time before, our kitty would look into it and would hiss and howl while following something around in it with her eyes. She'd leap off the back of the couch chasing after and clawing something in the room that wasn't visible to our eyes. Deeply terrorized, she found more solace in those days hiding under our bed.

The only place where I could occasionally have my own space was in the bathroom. After my shower, I felt a need to pray asking for a little extra help. As I sat there I saw a pair of grey, shadowy, translucent, footprints depressing the carpet on the opposite side of the door as if the carpet had been weighed down. The carpet would legitimately have been weighed down because light has mass and therefore has weight and it occupies space. The footprints would move and get more fidgety while the doorknob turned from left to right on the locked door escalating into a frantic pace. The door flexed as weight appeared to have been pressed against it. Whatever was on the other side of the door made a distracting racket while I prayed. I could no longer concentrate and wondered how my husband managed to continue sleeping. I found it obvious that prayer wasn't liked by these shadowy beings. The kid's behavior problems worsened and my husband, a probation officer, started using cocaine originally obtained from a nearby PD's evidence room.

I remember waking up intensely cold and found that a ceramic rabbit I had that initially faced me when I got into bed, had turned and appeared to be facing toward our bedroom's one and only window. I thought it odd but didn't devote any time investigating this because I was trying to keep to a very busy schedule. The next night I saw what looked like a very large toad on my dresser's hutch soundlessly watching me.

> It is written: "and I saw _three_ unclean spirits, like frogs, _come out of the mouth of the dragon/Reptilian,_ and out of the mouth of the beast, and out of the mouth of the false prophet. For they are the spirits of devils working miracles _which go forth unto the kings of the earth_ (the caulbearers and etc.) and of that whole world to gather them to the battle of that great day of God Almighty." (Revelation 16: 13-14)

The next night I found myself very cold again but unable to wake. I resolved myself to make a strong attempt to awaken should this happen again. In my sleep, on the _third_ night, I felt as if I was being watched as before. I struggled to open my eyes, finally, when I was able, I saw two very short Greys showing their faces just barely above my queen beds' footboard. Another Grey stood by my left side between my ankle and my knee, the same side the window was on. This one was taller than the thickness of me and both the mattress and box springs combined but not by much. Startled, the Grey pulled back opening its eyes even wider at the time because I had opened mine. The two smaller ones at the footboard bobbed their heads in what looked like an anxious anticipation. I couldn't keep my eyes open any longer and caught the last glimpse of the taller Grey's eyes resuming to normal while it started to lean toward me before I closed my eyes. I remember flying out of the window.

The following morning, when my husband woke me, he told me the floor was blanketed in frost on my side of the bed. I looked down and thought no wonder I was cold, the carpeting was indeed covered with a thick, white frost. When he exited the room, he left a trail of footprints seen in the melted frost. As with each of the previous days the ceramic rabbit faced the window. It is my feeling that three Greys came because that number may, in these cases, represent the infernal trinity thereby they mock the Holy Trinity.

In 2018 I listened to a video in which Yvonne Smith spoke of regressing abductees through hypnosis attending a UFO conference. They were on the schedule to be at a conference but found out after arriving that sometime soon the U.S. president, Bill Clinton, was expected to arrive. Usually, the secret service clears and area before a president arrives checking it out months in advance. One way in which they do this is to cancel events that may have previously been scheduled however, curiously, this UFO event hadn't been cancelled despite the fact that the secret service had already arrived and were seen relieving each other of their shifts in what appeared to have been in 20-minute intervals.

The VIPs at the UFO congress watched what they thought were four very unusual waiters stand by their table unlike the lack of attention given at the other tables. Their steadfast observance created an uncomfortable situation thereby dampening their flow information in what would be their normal exchange. After dining, two of her table guests (that she was made aware of) were followed back to their rooms.

Three couples associated with The Close Encounters Research Organization affiliated with Yvonne stayed on the third floor of the Village Inn Hotel on Coronado Island in San Diego, California. Having regressed them on the site, Yvonne found that on the first night all three couples had an experience. They remembered a bright light coming in through the window. The witnesses displayed signs of distress e.g. whimpering and trying to avoid the light they were seeing. The light became brighter. In one description a female was very upset and cried. She was heard to have been saying "no" repeatedly. Her roommate found that she had moved out of her bed and was huddled in the corner of the room by the closet. Her roommate said "be quiet…they won't see us". To have said this may have been an indication that they had some remembrance of having gone through this before. While huddled, they saw small beings that came through the window stating that they smelled like rotten eggs (Sulphur) akin to the odor many will say has been emitted by a Bigfoot or the "the black-eyed children". (Sulfur in the supernatural world is a key marker of demonic manifestation.) She continued to quell her roommate but it was too late, the Greys saw her, made direct eye contact, then backed up before abducting the huddled roommate.

In the days of Star Trek beaming a person or thing up is no longer fiction. In one of their television shows, the History Channel has shown that a particular frequency can dematerialize a person's body and transport it some distance away and, in addition, during this process our brain waves reach a maximum potential causing amnesia of the event.

The Greys were described as being opaque, small, smooth, and unborn-looking with large eyes. To the roommate that remained, it seemed that her acquaintance had been gone forever. She wasn't able to maintain her vigilance and fell back to sleep. She awoke when the light came back into their room; it was at the same time her roommate was brought back who now looked quite pale. Her first thought was that she was dead and, if she wasn't, she was very sick.

Screaming from the room next door was a man she met from the previous gathering. In her sickened, weakened voice she described his screams as animal-like. His wife was taken as well and when she was returned, she came back with a scoop mark and, underneath that mark, she had an implant. When she came back, she felt flu-like and achy. Perhaps this was because she may have had symptoms of the "bends" which could occur as it does from diving at great depths or from traveling in a fast ship and having been made to experience a difference in pressure. The man that screamed drew a picture of the Grey beings he saw. During the process of recalling the event, he seemed distressed having stated that he was upset and described the light he saw shining in his eyes coming from in between the blinds and the window as though it was a plane. Considering where the light emanated from it sounds very much like an interdimensional occurrence to me. While describing the event his voice started to quake, stating that they looked like shadows. He remembered thinking he wished it would just go away.

He could only see one clearly and described it as having a very large head, large and very black eyes, a very pointy chin, holes for a nose, and a line for a mouth. He remembered having a vibrating instrument put into his left ear and when he awoke there was blood on his pillow. He went to his doctor who told him he had a puncture mark in his ear. He continued to have a problem with his ear. A week after their stay in San Diego they continued to incur physical, unaccounted for anomalies primarily in the shape of triangles. Regarding the third party, it was found that the Greys were actually there for his wife; she had been levitated through the ceiling. Shortly thereafter she became pregnant with their daughter.

Through his regression, one of the men remembered that he had something done to his groin area and found that he had a triangular section of skin removed from his penis. Another male attendee had the same section of skin removed. It is believed that the UFO conference wasn't cancelled because they knew these particular UFO experiencers would be there. This appears to have been planned in order for them to experience this together. Part of their experience was being put into a tank that filled up with some sort of oxygenated fluid. They were made to breath in this fluid similar to what the Navy allegedly already has and what was in the movie "The Abyss" which assisted peoples' bodies to withstand pressure differences when reaching high speeds. Yvonne has had many other cases that have reported this same thing.

While lying there in deep thought I became aware of a strong wind rotating through the room in a clockwise direction which, in my world, means that something is attempting to pull something else up. Unable to move I laid there watching the silk plants yield to the direction the wind current was pulling them. The door was closed and so was the window in this, our recently constructed home. My husband came into the room, saw what was happening, shut the door, and walked away. Nice guy! The wind stopped shortly afterward.

The fourth night, after the initial encounter, I remember being walked up my hallway with a Grey holding each of my arms. I was brought to a German-looking woman wearing a lab coat. She was accusatory and used a very tough interrogation technique acting as though she knew everything about human behavior. I was calm through most of her interrogation correcting her false accusations as we went along. I had enough of her diatribe and took a swing (subtle) at her. I was grabbed simultaneously from behind. She ordered me to be put into a humiliating situation. She made sure to call out others to see me in that state attempting to intensify my intended humiliation. I didn't do what she expected and told her something I won't say here which seemed to gain her respect. In addition, I told her we'd have our day again and she wouldn't have the upper hand. Oddly she gave me what seemed to be a smile of acknowledgment then she quieted down. I was removed and don't remember anything else. I awoke laying across the width of the bed at its foot.

My husband became more distant and would get ready for the new day in the other bathroom while loading up on cocaine that I later became aware of. A pseudo busy guy, he apparently arranged for a hit on me having coerced one of his probationers to do his bidding. The probationer called our home, insulted me, then threatened to kill me. Weird that a guy I never saw in my life was able to attain the unlisted home phone number of a probation officer in those days or was it? On one other occasion, the probationer followed me into a store pretending to read a magazine while he watched me then followed me home despite my best driving tactics. I thought it would end while in route but it didn't. Not aware that he was able to follow me completely home, perhaps having been given my address in advance, a foot-chase ensued. I was in heels no less but I was still able to outsmart him.

It was near Thanksgiving and I was on my way home from work. I noticed the same car had been behind me for a couple of blocks. The woman driving parked in the middle of our alleyway about five car lengths behind me where I intended to park my car in our remote garage. Once parked I had to cross the alleyway taking the staircase to my home. While I walked across, I saw that she was trying to run me down; I made a mad dash to save my life. Later I found out that this was a woman my husband was more than friendly with at his work.

I was finally graduated at the top of my class which was pretty amazing considering. My professors thought I had a 99.9% chance of complete failure not even knowing the threats I faced. They only considered my age and my having children. Afterward, I got a job but lost it having to have two major surgeries nearly back to back after interfacing with the Greys. Was it because of what the Greys did to me? I have no way of knowing for sure but it is an odd coincidence if it was a coincidence at all.

My post-surgery midsection looked like it took a hit from a shotgun. Over time I couldn't believe how nicely I recovered from my wounds. Following my first surgery, after the Grey's visit and in writhing agony, I sat on the couch and noticed what I was later told was a chinch bug. They look like a small fly. My scalp felt as if it was moving and I found more in my hair. There were a few more on the couch, more on my shirt, on my pants and still more were crawling on my feet. Over by the fireplace there were some on the wall and as I looked even more covered the hallway walls. Sleeping at night I could feel them rustle on me and under the sheets. They were in the seams of the fitted sheet between the elastic and the sheet and were in all of my clothing including my undergarments, in my closet and dresser but none were in my husband's. I could feel them running around the tops of my legs between the elastic in my undergarment. Every part of my person had them. I was absolutely creeped out and wanted to go to a motel but couldn't. We became totally infested yet none of our adjoining neighbors had them. Vector Control told me they were attracted to light; which light I wondered? In horrendous pain, the seepage of blood, and the stretch of stitches, I screamed.

My husband set out to destroy the family we once had knowing that my daughters loved me. He succeeded. My daughters left to go live with their father. Before my youngest left, I photographed a picture of her by the fireplace; angry to be photographed, she exuded a large cloud of ectoplasm seen in the photograph I took of her. Their school would not permit my kids to go to another school that wasn't filled with gang activity and threats on their lives. Their situation at home with their step-father was too much to bear as were the continual paranormal experiences.

Our home went into foreclosure due to my husband's drug use and dalliances. Trying to do the Catholic thing and stick it out, we moved once again to the previous apartment complex whereupon I had a third surgery that I couldn't seem to heal from. My wound was finally cauterized, the blood accumulation was drained, and I was put into a very tight corset before I was coerced to go to work by my husband. The blood managed to soak prolifically through my clothes. We parted that day after he stated, "I don't think you'll die". Needless to say, he couldn't recognize his own clothes in his condition, a condition of his own choosing. Again, I must reiterate, that these beings destroy relationships in an attempt to isolate an abductee for their final abduction.

CHAPTER 7

They're Watching

By this time, I've been alone for quite some time and wanted someone to share my life with. I did a special ritual that allowed me to communicate with an archangel named Auriel. It was the first time I worked with her (feminine energy). Auriel had a sense of humor and made me laugh. The thought of her still brings a smile to my face.

I needed a few supplies to use in my temple work and drove to a recently opened metaphysical store. After a brief conversation with the proprietor I was followed out by a woman stating that she was a "Watcher". She said it was her job to watch me specifically. She said "you've always been loved by someone on the other side. He is a fearsome warrior and was a little on the dark side, well…maybe a little more than just a little. He was going to come to me really soon and would possess the body of a much younger man. He wanted to be with me soon. Within the second week of our conversation yes indeed, that man came into my life. We had wonderful years together; we were good for each other. He made me laugh again and I introduced him to many things he hadn't previously experienced. We were happy.

I talked him into going on a half-day fishing boat. It was near the days' end and we were experiencing rough seas. The boat was nearly on its side when I started to slide off the boat's engine cover, unable to get any traction. He reached over and was able to keep us both onboard; he saved my life.

As time ticked by, I started to look for someone I could permanently have in my life. One day after coming home from work I looked at my partner's face; there was something very different about it. The light in his eyes was gone. It was the person I knew alright but there was a definite difference; I would best describe it as an absence of an essence. I knew the warrior had gone. The possessed person and I have remained long-distance friends to this day. Shortly afterward I met someone.

CHAPTER 8

The Unfathomable is Founded in Reality

I n 2005 we retired within one of the many forests located in the Cascade Mountain Range in Oregon. The changing seasons and the peace that the wind brought as it rushed through the pines felt long overdue. We thought our souls and psyches needed a change of pace in our attempt to heal from the cities' gang violence. We decided that it was in our best interests to finally go out into the woods and validate the property's existence since it was something that I purchased from an ad despite my checking it out as best as I could prior to buying it. Our three acres looked enormous, perhaps it was how the land was parceled. As the years went by others that came over also thought the property looked huge. This was the first of many illusions to come.

When my husband and I first inspected the property; we located its survey markers and walked all over the property with someone whose job it was to show it. Of course, he made a heck of a racket as we walked just in case bears were in the vicinity. As we walked out to the N.E. corner, we found an amazing, polished, rectangular rock slab that was waist-high on me. If a man laid on this rock with his arms outstretched it would have fit him nicely. Keeping my thoughts to myself, my husband, who hadn't looked into or read what I had blurted out, "that's an altar!". After hearing his comment, I quickly jerked a bit having noted that even he, recognized it as an altar.

We made a second trip there and took some of his family with us. We were excited at the prospect of building our home and living in peace away from constant gunfire and crime in the state we currently lived in, moving to an affordable area that we felt was suitable for retirement. We noticed that the one-piece, thought-to-be-an-alter was now gone. We were finally in a position to relocate but still wondered how something weighing several tons could go missing. No matter, the wheels of progress were in motion.

I returned to Oregon by myself. My husband planned to live in California in a different location another two years before he thought he'd retire in an attempt to better his retirement package. I lived in a motel for the time having procured a contractor to start the project of our modest but comfortable home. Our contractor stated that he was a Water Witch. He chose where the well would be by sticking a stick into the ground. By doing so he picked the best well in the area at a depth of less than 80 feet which was unheard of for that area and the neighboring areas as well.

Our contractor had a stellar reputation but building the house didn't go well. Taking things into consideration we had the normal issues popup until a point wherein they seemed far from normal. In addition, our map indicated that there was a stream in the back of our property but the map was incorrect; it was actually on the property in back of ours.

We purchased what was once Native American land. It was their tradition to pass it down to the head-of-household which, I was. The area experienced volcanic activity in at least one point in its history. The silica soil was deadly in some spots; it had the characteristics of quicksand. A truck standing for less than 10 minutes in places would sink into the earth. As each season passed there was another relatively substantial mound our dip somewhere due to the grounds' constant movement. Fortunately for us, our house stood on rock.

I would use our metal detector at times as a form of recreation. It would indicate a particular thing, we'd dig, then it would indicate something else or nothing at all. No matter where we used it; we constantly received faux readings.

After we moved in, we found out that if we walked further than our property-line, in the back of the adjacent lot toward the N.E., we came upon a shack that an employee for the ranch two lots in back of us attempted to build. The shanty was on bare ground and there were spaces in-between the wall and the ceiling boards. I've experienced temperatures dipping to -14 degrees and the shack had no heat source. There were two, thick supporting boards holding up planks for a makeshift bed. A sinking feeling set in when we saw a small coral made for a child which would have barricaded him/her from leaving as well as tiny little shoes that a two-year-old would wear ground into the dirt. Later we found out that the rancher this employee worked for was a pedophile. The point I'm attempting to make is that UFO sightings and the paranormal activity that surrounds them have a negative impact on either the people near them, their surroundings, or both.

The vicinity in which we lived was referred to as "The Wild West". A war started to develop between the rancher and myself. The rancher tried to dupe me into believing my land was open range and, at the time, he already succeeded in bluffing the Sheriff. I showed the Sheriff the legal documents straightening him out.At one time the rancher before this one and his crew at this same ranch broke into the local's homes using chainsaws. Because of budget cuts we were given a notice that there would be no law enforcement assistance during a certain period of each night and day making everyone in the area fair game for the unscrupulous. Self-defense became our priority. The Sheriff himself told us to make sure everything was locked and if we had an issue to take care of it ourselves. We heard that there were many bodies buried with a backhoe in these parts, consequently, we became as tough as the area required.

I tried to be on location when the workmen were at the house and, as they were in and out so much, I left the front door unlocked for them. While doing some things inside the home I heard one workman pound on the front door. I thought to myself, "why isn't he coming in"? Going over to the door I found that it was locked.

He asked that I not lock the door. I promptly responded, "I had it unlocked, but I don't understand, what happened"? As his response, he gave me one of "those looks" mixed with a little frustration and anger. The doors continued to lock themselves. It got so bad that I had to carry my keys around with me especially because I was out in the middle of nowhere; the guys were gone at times, and cell phone reception was spotty at best.

As a consequence, I blessed and saged (burned Sage) the house and performed a small ritual asking the Lord of the Earth to protect it. I made a grievous error; I wrote the Lord's name (on a large flat man-made stone near the outside wall of the kitchen window). His name's last letter didn't indicate a final" letter which would have been written differently than it would have if it was placed in the middle of a word. Because I didn't take this into account the letter represented infinity so now it looked like the Lord of the Earth would preside over my home forever.

On the second day, I actually started occupying the home. My furniture still hadn't arrived; that would be a while yet. I had one chair, a lamp, and a television in my possession. I only received one station before we procured the Internet. The TV show I was able to watch was funny beyond belief and I looked forward to viewing it as often as I could. Oddly, very oddly now that I think about it, it was a show whose main characters were wooden, oversexed, space puppets. Our security lights weren't in but fortunately the blinds were.

Absorbed in my T.V. show I heard a bipedal, deliberate stomping on the patio. It was as though a very heavy sledge hammer, wrapped in terry cloth, thudded down onto the concrete. I'm mentioning terry cloth because the sledge hammer-like walking didn't have a "clink" sound like a sledgehammer would have on a hard patio's surface. To hear the sound of this perceived immense weight walking about resonating through this stone-like surface was unnerving. It was pitch-black out in the forest and at the time; I had no form of defense with me which made things more unsettling. I couldn't possibly imagine what weighed so much that could be bipedal. I made my way to the glass sliding door and pulled the blind slat slightly apart with my finger trying to take a look outside. I couldn't see anything under the present conditions. Standing on the inside, but, on the outside of the glass door, I heard <u>three</u> heavy-handed hand slaps on the glass. Whatever it was had a fantastic sensing ability because the hand slaps were about where the level my head was. I knew that on the last slap whatever it was left its hand there for a longer duration than for the other slaps. Afterward, whatever it was, left toward the lot where the altar had been. I stood there shaking, hoping that it wouldn't be back again.

Up until this time, when I went out front, I'd see the rock I wrote on. It was exactly where I placed it, then… it vanished the day after the bipedal walk on the patio. I took a large shovel and dug deep into the area but never found the stone with the "Lord of the Earth's name on it that I wrote in Hebrew. Perhaps what walked onto the patio recognized, needed, or wanted it.

At long last my furniture arrived; much of it was damaged. The only repair man sent out by the mover's insurance company in this dysfunctional town came out to give an estimate for the repairs. While out at our home he said he had too many personal problems and as such he wouldn't make any repairs. During this time my husband would take the train to visit off and on attending to some chores that needed to be done like putting up ceiling fans or working on so many other projects.

The Summer heat was nearly unbearable. One day, in July, it reached 121 degrees. The heat lingered even at night with the exception of about one or two hours as I lay there sweating through the sheets. My hair became wringing wet; I wondered why the heck I listened to the woman that sold the home when she stated that it was cooler out where we lived and that we didn't need an air-conditioner.

As the place started to take shape, I got the hose in the front yard and started to wash off the immediate area. I remained relatively motionless while watching a puma advance toward me but none-the-less I was captivated by its grace and poise. Studying it, it appeared to look very much like hologram. The cougar was placid in its appearance and movements. I could see its weight release onto its paws as its toes spread out from under its weight. The cat proceeded to walk up to me vanishing without aggression within ten feet. I looked up the word "puma" and, according to native culture, it was supposed to have meant "courage"; mine was tested that day. For some strange reason that I can't explain, during the whole event, I was able to maintain "a calm". I wasn't sure what had happened at that time but I knew it was something that would stay with me forever.

Since the puma appeared as a hologram I wondered if it could have been a product of Project Blue Beam or if it was from accumulated residual energy in the area. The puma appeared on a clear-sky-day so I wouldn't have noticed Project Blue Beam in operation with my naked eye.

> *Serge Monast, a self-styled journalist from Quebec (according to Wikipedia) wrote an influential paper in 1994 called "Project Blue Beam". In his paper, he alleged that both NASA and the United Nations have worked on simulating an invasion from space using holograms.*
>
> *In "The Sunday Express", by Jon Austin which was published Wednesday, January 18, 2017, in what looked like an apparition seen by thousands, was a floating city in the skies of Yueyang, China. The event sparked claims of being given a glimpse into another dimension. This particular <u>hologram</u> was the latest at the time in a series of so-called floating cities seen across the globe that were most often seen in China.*
>
> *Since then I have read other articles e.g. regarding the tactical usefulness of Project Blue Beam, one of which was to deceive the enemy attempting to make them think that armored vehicles were approaching when there were none and two, that of Blue Beams' plausible use in crowd control and acts of deception among other plausible control uses. As you can see that whether technology is new or ancient it has the full capability of influencing and or amending religion as we have known it integrating it with falsehoods.*

The insanity continued. Every day, for the first three months of occupancy, a black unmarked helicopter arrived. It would either hover, usually on the S.E. wall of our bedroom, or it would circle the house from forty-five minutes through one hour without fail. Rarely would it position itself on the E. wall of our bedroom but, when it did, it hovered above the pines (because the pines were blocking any further descent) positioning itself to enable its occupants to look into the bedroom window. Infuriated, I went outside and gave them an unwelcoming hand gesture for some duration.

After the appearances of the black, unmarked helicopter were at the end of its <u>three</u>-month surveillance a very small, two-man helicopter came and hovered low over the Sage Brush in the front yard about 175 feet from the house. The second person, the passenger, sported a broad grin, and was dressed in khaki pants and a light-colored shirt. He draped his right leg out of the chopper getting ready to jump onto the ground. After all that had occurred any stranger was suspect and I let him know just how welcome he was while I stood there with my rifle on the porch waving him off. Seeing my game-face he found it in their best interest(s) to hurriedly remove themselves from the property that had "no trespassing" signs all over it. The two men were never seen again or at least in my conscious memory.

My husband decided to move up sooner than he planned bringing our other kitty with him. My beloved furball held a grudge against me for two years thinking that I left her behind. At about this time I started to hear noises in the house after purchasing a pressed wood rocking chair from a collectible store. We'd hear its rocking and creaking sounds in our bedroom, hand slapping on my jewelry box, kitchen cupboard doors slamming, and something springing off of a sofa table that we had photographs on including antique family photos and a flower arrangement. As this continued, some nights were worse than others. My husband asked "are you hearing those noises at night, I think the cat broke something"; the kitties weren't anywhere near the noises, they were on our bed with us.

The kitties would often freeze in place, both looking terribly frightened, starring at the rocking chair in our room when it acted up. From time to time I thought my cat jumped on the bed and would walk on me and so did my husband. He'd reach over to pet our cat that loved to be loved but she wasn't there. The pressure points distributing its weight from its feet hurt. We would sit up from time to time, still feeling something stand on us but neither of us saw anything. I've come to conclude that when there is something undesirable around it can change its form to what it feels will be an acceptable form thereby gaining acceptance, avoiding the circumstance of being banished/expelled. Both of my cats dashed off the bed in a hurry when "whatever" it was, came near them on our bed.

We started to have a problem with the lighting in the dining and living rooms. The light shut out and we couldn't turn it back on. The security lights in the backyard would surpass their preset shutoff times after having flicked on. There were no insects or moths to activate them. I intentionally hid behind the wall in the house to catch the light going on. It would turn off when I tried to see what was turning it on. The game of cat and mouse continued until I gave up trying to catch it.

I went to get my camera and Ovilius. I saw that "whatever" was there seemed to have originated from or may have come from either the bathroom mirror or the grounds behind the bathroom mirror's wall where the Bigfoot footprint was found. I traced its path moving from the area of the bathroom mirror to the side of the bed where I sleep, over to the living room couch, then the dining table before it backtracked to an oil painting I had in the entry. The oil painting was that of a Native American child. The entity stayed there for a while; it had been cornered. I took a picture and in it you can see a being that seems to be emerging from it. It has a narrow forehead with furrow lines on its brow, a bulbous jaw and nose, a slit for a mouth, and large round black eyes.

I originally purchased this picture in a collectible store. It had been in a heap of what seemed to be dirty junk on the ground. The seller told me that its previous owner was eating spaghetti with his family. He was staring at the picture, stood up, said nothing, then threw his plate of spaghetti at it. His family was pretty mortified at his outburst. He ripped the painting off of the wall and brought it into the collectible shop throwing it onto the floor. The question is, had he been steadily seeing something in the painting until he finally had enough?

We were out of state on vacation and took a picture of a petroglyph of what I call a frog person. You can see it near the picture's bottom left and there is another small one in the middle row. Note that they appear with what seem to be robotic creations, those that look like ant people, and what may be thought of as a spacecraft. There is also what looks like a small cap-shaped UFO. It looks like it has thrust coming from under it or perhaps the lines indicate an upward movement.

The being in the oil painting looks similar to that in the petroglyph drawing. The indigenous people on Easter Island have found an identical image in their caves and call these frog beings "the Watchers".

For three days afterward, when we came back from vacation, the house smelled hygienic akin to a hospital but not quite. It gave off a different but a clean fragrance unlike alcohol. I often wondered if a hospital had been set up there at one time during the Indian wars. My Ovilus would speak of two graves in a particular spot and the killing of a pastor by Indian soldiers. Time after time I'd take the Ovilus out to this same spot and it would faithfully repeat the tale. It mentioned the pastor's name at one time, I fact checked it, but by this time I have forgotten it. At the time I mentioned it to a friend of mine. He was well aware of Oregon's history in these parts. He heard tell of the pastor. He verified that he was killed by the Indian soldiers which corroborated with what the Ovilus said. In this area, the Modoc engaged in a war with the U.S. Army from 1872 through 1873. Fort Klamath was roughly 40 miles from our home.

Did a porthole open up or was it opened up on this once Indian land brought about by the ceremonies they performed, was it something else, or was it a combination of things? I didn't think so at the time but considering encountering black, unmarked helicopters that came when I moved in, in conjunction with what appeared to be paranormal (peternormal) activity, I wondered! In addition, I also pondered if a new/test technology wasn't being employed in this remote area far away from prying eyes. The property was roughly 60 miles from the Kingsley Field Air National Guard Base. There was a segment of their base containing highly guarded, secret, quonset buildings. A woman I met had a boyfriend in the Air Force that worked at the base. She said she knew more about UFOs than she wanted to and didn't want to hear any more about them from her boyfriend. Quite frankly, she was scared.

Late, in October around the 21st, 2014, I was compelled to go outside around midnight to take a picture. I aimed my camera in the direction where I felt a presence. It was too dark for me to see anything. The next morning I found I took a picture of an Archquloid. Ironically, I took it on the side of the house where a Bigfoot footprint was found and other anomalies have manifested. I awoke the next morning in pain. Brushing back my nightgown sleeves; I saw a bright-pink burn on the tops of each of my arms from about 2" below my elbow to the middle knuckle on each hand. The burn lasted for about three weeks; it never blistered.

It is alleged that the Ebens (Greys with a more rounded chin) dwell on the planet Serpo and have created the Archquloids in a rapid cloning cycle. They are said to have presented two or more of them to the U.S. Government for study and observation. Both the Archquloids and Ebens are said to have landed at Holloman Airforce Base

*New Mexico, on April 25,1964. They presented them at
the time of Eisenhower's visit.*

Due to the photograph's pixels, I was unable to have a
reproducible, book printable copy of the photograph so I drew the
image instead and it is quite accurate. I found it interesting that she
is nude but was wearing a headscarf. Could it be, that because of this,
we may be so preoccupied with nudity that we don't relegate much
importance to what could be masked e.g. the back of the head, the
brain's stem, and her larynx?

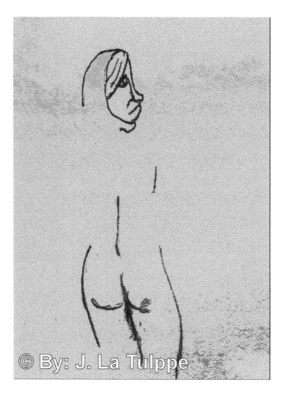

By now my Ovilius had become a standard part of my
equipment. Because it is such a time-consuming process, I am
reluctant to go through my records and won't jot down the date of
this event which occurred in this series. It was quite cold outside and
again I was awakened by electromagnetic energy, feeling compelled

to go outside and to take a picture around the time period from midnight through 2:30 in the A.M. For some reason I can't get the printer to print the entire picture which would have shown its neck that would have indicated that it was sweeping down from the sky to our home. This does not look like a typical Reptilian; it looks like it may have been a Draco Reptilian.

I took the photo to a MUFON symposium and showed it to a Polish journalist. He believed it has been the only photo taken that shows a demon (likely an interdimensional Reptilian) with an orb. He has always known that orbs are the minions of these beings. The protrusions on its head are supposed to be scaly protrusions and not horns. Hopefully, you've noticed that there are protrusions on the head of the wax impression of the Reptilian that was found on the reversal candle shown previously in this text. The orb is hovering over the area that had the impression of the Bigfoot footprint and was nearby to the Annumiki footprints. The Annumiki prints gave off exceptionally high E.M. and trimeter readings. The readings lead from there to the side of my bed. In addition, very close to the time I moved from there, I took my bionic ear (listening device) outside and, walking toward that side of the house, I pointed it straight up and listened to what sounded like tormented human cries. I don't feel that this was residual energy stored in the rocks under and around the home. I aimed the bionic ear toward the ground and didn't hear anything. The sounds came from above me and again, on that same wall. where our headboard was and where, at one time, a vortex opened up nearby.

I went outside with my husband to show him what the Ovilius previously said. It replicated what it always had in the same areas divulging the same historic and relevant information but this time, when I asked it what the name of the demon was, it said and printed out an exceptionally long name. I can't emphasize enough how bizarre my husband acts when he's frightened by these events. I asked that he be quiet but he spoke nervously and repetitiously throughout all that was relayed so I couldn't hear its name or to have been able to record it.

The photo of what looks like a Draco Reptilian was forwarded to a person associated with the UFO Digest. Below is a comment made by the photos' analyst:

> George Filer
> Today at 5:48 PM
> ██████████████ asked me to forward this message
> to you
> Regards, George Filer
> From: ████████████████
> Sent: Saturday, March 22, 2014 9:17 PM
> To: George Filer
> Cc: ████████████████
>
> Subject: Re: Filer's Files #12 2014–Dr. Roger Leir Passes, Annunaki and Human Origins, Moon Map Cylinder

Dear Major,

Thank you for your newsletter.

I was impressed by the Orb photo submitted by Jeanette La Tulippe, so I conducted some of my "Gamma Whammy" to enhance the image and enlarged them. One highlighted the blue green light and revealed the depth. I then reversed Red and Blue colors (mstar enh-rxb) that produced the orange-yellow effects.

It appears to me that the floating globular shape could have been the result of the moonlight's refraction by some sort of translucent aerosol, like a ball of moist gas <not "Swamp Gas"...., but something more "ectoplasmic" more in common with ghost experiences and some <u>alien intrusions</u>. Genies and demons are often described as gaseous in nature and with the ability to congeal and shape shift into various shapes. This could be one such sample.

Please share these with Ms. La Tulippe.

Warm regards,

In another account, I was sitting on the couch while Ron was busy fixing lunch in the kitchen when I turned and exclaimed, "what the hell is that?" On the rise, in the front yard, white spirals were coming out of the ground that were five feet tall; some were just a little bit taller. I slipped on my shoes and grabbed the Ovilius and camera. Having climbed up a smaller hill I looked to my left feeling that something was there but I couldn't see anything. I kept pacing the wire fence until I decided to move upward, moving toward the next incline. I saw nothing then came back down the hill. I rechecked the same area. There was a milky looking, rough chiseled in its appearance, bell-shaped craft that had bands on the bottom of it. I could see through its edge on my left. I moved up toward the top of the hill to see if I could get a better shot but a vehicle started to come up the main road. I knew I blew the opportunity to take the shot. I came back down but now the craft which had been under the electrical lines appeared to be gone. I salvaged what I could of the situation taking pictures of the area from different standpoints. The results were the same from all of the perspectives. The needles on the pines looked extruded, the branches they were on looked twisted, and there was some pink in the coloring of the foliage. I felt that something huge was advancing toward me, fearful, I dropped back but still kept taking pictures of the area. I thought that "whatever" I couldn't see was still around. The final pictures showed its advancement through the distortions listed above as they did in the final shot where I thought the "whatever" was standing. Because I was sensing the "whatever", I knew it was really tall. My fear intensified substantially so I walked a wide circle around this thing, passing in between the fence's wires before finally getting into my house. When I saw what I photographed I physically shook for over one hour. The picture I posted below is not the same incident but the white stuff coming out of the ground looks like what was up on the hill with the exception that this white stuff is too short and they do not spiral.

Sometime later Charles Hall told me that the bands on the bottom of the craft were what the forcefield was activated through and its surface helped in avoiding radar. He stated that when the craft looked as it did (milky) is when it was the most dangerous to be around because it is either cloaking or uncloaking. Afterward, I brought my camera into the camera shop and was told that only E.M. energy could make the pictures I took appear as they did.

I asked to meet with the local tribal/heritage person from the Modoc tribe hoping that he had some insight and would share his knowledge with me. We met at a local café for lunch. He told me that one day he and his son were standing on the main road that ran through our small town which only consisted of a few buildings. They saw a silvery 10' diameter orb-shaped object hovering about 10' off of the road. They continued to watch it soundlessly hover above the road for a while until it flew off. He mimicked its angular assent with the wave of his arm. At some other time, he went hunting with his friends on one of the three buttes that they considered sacred and where many of their religious ceremonies had taken place. While they walked along, he looked up into the night sky and saw that the stars were blocked out by a soundless, triangular shape that seemed miles wide that he said was way out in space. Abruptly he interjected with "there's a war out there; it blew up, there was a flash of a bright white light in the center of the craft then all of its illumination turned black from the center of the craft extending to its outermost edges before it finally exposed the stars that were previously masked by its size". The nighttime forest turned into day and he could see all of the animals and watched the rabbits as they ran. Rather than blowing up, this may have been its propulsion system whisking the craft away.

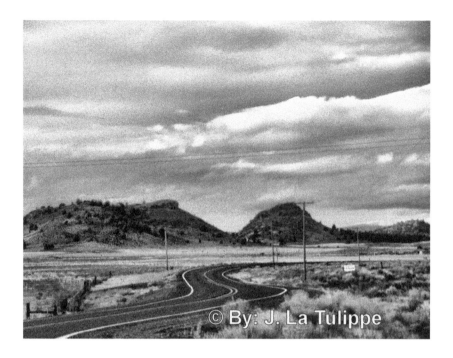

© By: J. La Tulippe

I told him about the previous goings-on at my house, the bruises, triangular burn, fluorescent markings, and following these, the additional, nearly side-by-side, barefoot footprints on the side of the house. I told him what the Ovilius said about them which described them in detail and it even spoke about Don. The Ovilius said that he killed his enemies in the Springtime.

More about Don: Living in the mountains, we had to take regular mini vacations; we were starved for entertainment. This time we were headed for Virginia City, Nevada. For those that haven't been there, Virginia City is an old silver mining town with quite a history. We went to a bar to grab a hotdog for lunch and met Mississippi, a bartender there. For some reason, acting out of her character, she looked at me and gave me a reading right then and there. Folks thought it was quite odd because they hadn't known her to do such things much less to have that ability. I wondered if something unusual hadn't spoken through her. In a portion of her reading, she said that I have a relative named Don. He was much younger and liked me very much. She said he was around me. I don't know much about my family history none-the-less I thanked her and soon afterward we were on our way back home.

It was quite late when we got back. The house was filled with an enveloping and seductive fragrance completely unmatched by anything known today. It emanated from above the valance from one of the two living-room windows. I headed into the shower; by now my husband was fast asleep. I heard a beautiful melody coming from somewhere in the house. I exited the shower, wrapped myself up into a towel taking my Ovilius with me, and walked about until I reached the back of the couch on the side where I usually sit. The E.M. meter's light registered a bright red at this spot. Stopping, I asked the Ovilius what it was that I heard. It replied "a simple melody". I asked who was playing it and it said "Don". I couldn't say anything further; I was at a loss for words but I did thank Don for his music. I wished he would have played for me again at another time; his music was that nice.

The native told me that they had another being out there besides Bigfoot called "the little people". They're about two feet through five feet tall and are hairy. The other word they had for the "little people" were the Annumiki. To the extent that I was able to research this word, it is Algonquin and these Annumiki are associated with the Thunderbird along with their fire and lightning in the sky. The Thunderbird may, in fact, be the native's description of a UFO as ancient alien theorists believe.

I recall being told that there are people that park along the road leading toward the nearby Bly Mountain for the sole purpose of watching UFOs. In this Bigfoot sighting area, some families have watched UFOs for years.

I asked the Native about the highly polished altar we saw when we first arrived just off of our lot to the North. He said it was theirs alright. All of their stone altars had been polished. He said that they did everything on these altars e.g. weddings, births, etc. I then asked, what other things were done; he refused to answer. He asked me if the altar sat on top of rocks. To be honest I couldn't recall. I did see some rocks around its parameter up against its sides, not a great deal of them but some. After telling him this he showed signs of being afraid and wanted to leave immediately. I wondered if the altar had been on rocks if it would have been some form of imprisonment or perhaps a gravesite. After our conversation, he told me that he would meet with the Elders and would tell them what we discussed.

Sensing electromagnetic energy again, I found myself becoming fully alert which was usually around midnight through 2:00 A.M. We had an atomic clock and, as usual during these events, the clock would either advance or it would go back one hour. I didn't think this was too peculiar until I researched what it took for an atomic clock to do this.

> It has been said that the speed of Light is the speed limit of the universe. In "Special Relativity" Einstein proved that the faster one travels the slower time ticks for a person actually sending the person into the future. However, in "General Relativity", Einstein proved that gravity is actually an acceleration due to the curvature of space-time. The speed of light still can't be exceeded but you can theoretically arrive at your destination before light reaches it if a shortcut is taken through curved space. This allows for time travel to the past without violating relativity.
>
> Large masses, like planets, warp the fabric of outer-space. Once warped, it allows for the possibility of wormholes, and exotic propulsion.

At our residence we tried to take every precaution we were aware of for our safety and one of them was to put dowels in our window channels. One night I awoke, hearing laborious, heavy walking through our bedroom doorway at a relatively fast pace. Not that this may be the case but I've evidenced this type of labored walking from a demonic source in the past. I sprang upward hearing the heavy plantation blinds thrashing and the dowel hitting the window and its frame. My mind tried to make sense out of what was going on thinking that this must be taking place from the outside of the window because I couldn't see anything in front of the window (on my side) altering the blinds nor could I see the dowel move yet the sounds indicated both were moving. The sounds indicated that whatever was moving the blinds and dowel was extremely frustrated. I thought perhaps a hand reached around from the opposite side. Of course, the dowel was on the inside of the window so that couldn't be it. Was the window punched through so that this could be done? Then, something overcame me, I don't know what; I put my head down and immediately fell asleep.

The next morning, we saw that the dowel had been lifted, the window was open, and the blinds were askew. Two things had occurred in the event that took place, 1. there was some sort of a time delay so that the event couldn't be seen in its current time and at least two beings had to be present, one to stir the blinds and one to put me out. I've heard that in alien or MILAB abductions, they are able to put people out with the use of a special spray they have.

© By: J. La Tulippe

After I found my window opened, I happened upon an article written by Derrel Sims, Chief Investigator of UFO Abductions for the Houston UFO Network.

> "Derrel discovered unusual fluorescent markings on numerous abductees claiming that they had alien contact. The primary fluorescence found on abductees following an abduction appeared in the yellow-green region of the visible spectrum. The sites found on the body included portions of the arms, shoulders, ears, breasts, legs, hands, chin, chest and even inside the mouth. Most of the fluorescence was subdermal which means that it couldn't be rubbed or cleaned off. In one case, a dime-sized marking on the palm of a hand was rigorously massaged; its fluorescence diffused into the massaged areas of the hand and fingers, however, it continued to remain subdermal. A reddish-pink fluorescence was discovered on the hands, fingers, palms, and neck regions of an abductee who recalled handling and cuddling an alien/human, infant (hybrid) during her encounter. White fluorescence was found in the mouth, oral mucous membranes, and tongue. Blue fluorescence was observed on the hands, and on the arm in an unusual heart-shaped Mandelbrot design. In general, most of the fluorescence was found to be an irregular splotching. All fluorescence was seen using a commercially available UV (short and long wave) blacklight source in a darkened area. Most fluorescence faded within one to four days following the alleged alien encounter." It was noted that when an implant/chip had been inserted, a temporal fluorescence may have lasted for several weeks.

I wondered if I had experienced a dream or if I really experienced something else. Months earlier I bought a blacklight. I took it out of its case and shut out the light in the bathroom examining myself to see if anything unusual had occurred. You can see in the photo below that I had a yellow-green fluorescence on my nose. It looked like a line was put into my right nostril. Using the blacklight I saw that the fluorescence continued inside of my nostril for as far as I could see. This same day I also sent for a hematite bracelet.

During the (roughly) five days that passed I had another unsettling dream. I remember part of it; I may be blocking the rest. I awoke with a matching pair of bruises, one on each of my inner thighs.

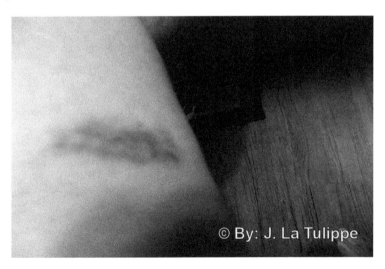

The following morning I heard my husband scream from the bathroom. He said so many things in his horror, most of which I won't repeat but one of the others was "I have the same bruises you do".

After the morning he got his bruises I woke up with a triangular (3 sided) burn on my left hand. The burn was raised in relief into a perfect triangle off of the rest of my hand. Since we generally hold our hands down this may represent the inverted triangle.

> "Fluorescent markings such as the crescent, _triangle_, and heart-shaped Mandelbrot appeared as if they were deliberate designs or 'brands' on certain individuals."

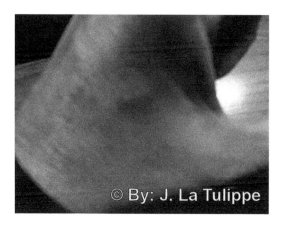

Later that same day my hematite bracelet I sent for arrived. I put it on and the beginnings of my thumb down to near its base continually throbbed day after day for the following few days until the bracelet disappeared. I wore it continually. It was on after I took my bath however I woke up without it. We looked everywhere and couldn't find it. My thumb stopped throbbing when the bracelet was off. If I was implanted, I'm sure the implant has traveled or perhaps it was removed and relocated. I looked at an x-ray on-line and saw that someone appeared to have been implanted in the same spot. Hematite is somewhat similar to magnetite and is supposed to hamper their propulsion system.

On September 19, 2016, while in bed and without going into detail, I felt as though I was being touched. On the 20th my husband was in bed and thought I was standing by his bedside stroking his face when in fact I was in the bathtub. He was scared when he found out it wasn't me. I took photos of our room but nothing materialized. I took out the Ovilus; its E.M. reading was a consistent red inside and outside of our home. Having a red reading for the outside of our home stunned me. It was unusual to have both areas in the red. The last time I did this there were interdimensional beings in the area. Since I was in my jammies and, without cover, I didn't venture into the woods. The Ovilius also said Poppa (I looked up the words' definition on 9/20/16 and found that it means: who's your daddy). It is also a word used by people that have been taken into the MK Ultra program and is the name of their owner or keeper. I tried to explain to my husband what was going on when his face got stroked. "Whatever" was around was referring to me when the text on the Ovilius read "witch, bury now". Obviously, something was angry knowing that I was aware of their presence as I dutifully tried to inform my husband that he was in danger. The Ovilius started making a noise that I don't know how to describe except that it reminded me of a fast-paced Geiger counter. It was fairly consistent in its rhythm except it deviated just once. I didn't think it was capable of making this noise.

I also did a remote view that I called in on a radio show. Their trusted medium said that I was highly psychic but after she gave it more thought she said I may be a really good medium instead. Personally, I believe I'm both.

On October 6, 2016, we were on our way back home from a mini-vacation and were traveling on the 140 out of Lakeview toward Oregon. Between 6:30 thru 7:00 P.M. I saw a black, matt, dumbbell object that was a nickel through quarter-sized at arm's length. The ends of the dumbbell were a perfect cube. A few days earlier a dumbbell-shaped flying object was seen in New Jersey although it was much smaller and its style was different. The sky in this open area was a dull matt however there was a brilliant "S" shaped cloud that was miles high. I was unable to capture all of it.

The other clouds came and went but this "S" remained for hours until it was nearly sunset. The top portion of it was the first to wear off.

At first, I was dumbfounded when I looked at the flying, black mat dumbbell. I finally told my husband about it who was driving at the time while reaching down to the floorboards trying to retrieve my camera out of my purse (a project in itself). While having my camera in hand I aimed it at the object. We passed by a rock wall that had been blasted to make the road. These stone blockages seemed to be located at fairly regular intervals. I turned to get a shot out of the back window but it was nowhere to be seen. Now that we were home, the "S" was no longer in the sky. I heard that people psychically called in UFOs. I thought no harm done and tried it for myself. At around 9 P.M., when it was pitch black out, the cloud was there again shimmering against the black sky in the S.E.

I needed to take a mental break and stood in my kitchen looking out of the window and enjoyed watching the jackrabbits running across the drive and bald eagles soar when, unexpectedly, I saw an odd object. It was what is described today as a cigar shaped craft. Watching how the sunlight reflected off of its surface it seemed dented all over from my point of view. At the time it appeared to be traveling the same speed as a regular passenger jet so I thought I'd move over to the adjacent room and continue to view it from our home's office knowing I could have seen it from there if it continued its present speed. When I reached the other room, it was either gone or it appeared to have been gone.

My husband and I often found the need to get out of town especially after long, isolating Winters and, in August, we headed up North to see the 205-foot-tall Heceta Head Lighthouse.

Our scenic day was nearly at an end; it was time to travel Southward toward home. The Oregon coast is wild, rocky, and quite treacherous; its ocean's waves are completely unpredictable. Before going home, we thought we would walk down the dirt path toward the beach looking for photo opportunities. On the way down we saw a captivating bridge. This was a blustery day and it wasn't unheard of to have 200 m.p.h. winds in this area. Back in the day, ropes were tied from the lighthouse to its surrounding buildings so people could hang on while walking so they wouldn't be blown away especially the women with their long, flowing skirts. While walking toward the bridge I looked up and saw what is defined as a "fish-cracker" shaped UFO. Stunned I called out to my husband and said: "do you see how big that damn thing is?" Filled with what seemed like an immediate urgency to leave, hearing the stress in his voice, he said, "let's go, let's go". Despite strong winds, the object was unwavering, was white in color, and it was soundless. He continued urging me to leave immediately. I already took a picture of the bridge with a whiteish sky. When I got home, I found that I did capture the UFO in my bridge picture. I altered the undertones in the picture to bring out the image from its surroundings. Its image is in the upper left.

© By: J. La Tulippe

© By: J. La Tulippe

Tired, he asked that I drive until we got home. Something strange happened when we rose to the top of the road once crossing the spot on the bridge that had been nearly under the UFO.

The 101 highway is a winding road. If you can imagine riding on the back of a sidewinder snake then you will understand what it is to drive on that road. Shortly after we reached the top and were on our way again, my windshield turned white. I did everything I could to clear it like opening the windows, wiping inside of the window, and using my wiper blades on the outside but nothing worked not even for a second. Mortified I told my husband "I'm blind, I'm completely blind. I knew the cliff's edge was to my right and every few seconds I'd be into another turn, a turn I couldn't see. I couldn't see any oncoming cars nor the cars next to me even with my window rolled down. My husband, usually a hyper man, acted oddly. He acknowledged my not being able to see but said you'll be all right then laid his head back and went immediately to sleep. My only means of navigation was to keep my widow down and to drive strictly by listening to the sound of the other vehicles. My heart pounded loudly and I could hear the rush of my own blood in my ears. Hearing the other cars and trucks whiz past me I wondered why the other drivers could see and I couldn't. Very suddenly the windshield cleared and I saw that I navigated miles through this meandering maze without hitting another vehicle or worse, driving off of the cliff.

After arriving home, before I did anything else, I ran into the house and turned on the news. The news reported that others in the area where we were reported seeing a UFO in the same area that we took the fish-cracker shaped UFO picture. A couple of days afterward a wasp UFO was seen in Northern California.

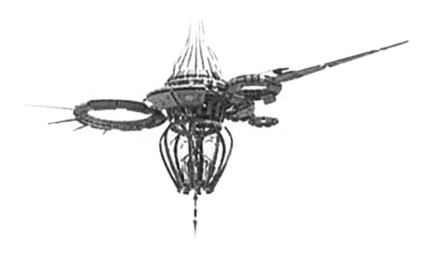

In November we got our satellite dish put in. It was morning and my husband was in the bathroom washing up. I was walking near the bedroom window when I shouted, "Come quick, we're on fire". He ran over to see what I was talking about. Together we watched a white smoke-like substance oozing out of the tiny tip of a Juniper leaf. It was traveling in a South-Eastern direction. The substance started to morph, and, as a result, the two of us ran out to the Juniper tree watching this thing get considerably larger until it was approximately 15' long and about 6' thick. It's finished shape looked like an elongated Cumulus Nimbus Cloud. Despite the fact that there was no wind, it made a U-turn. It moved toward the North traveling roughly five feet above our heads, then, another, and another, and still another cloud came out of the same place on the tree, all recreating the same movements as the first object, moving toward the North until approximately six of them were all Northbound one behind the other as if in formation. It was strange to see these forms move. It was as though they were being directed by an intelligence or that they were the intelligence.

Years later, while getting my hair done in the nearby Native American community, I inquired as to what the clouds may have really been. One woman, anxious to relay the information told me, "I know what they are, they are called fish"! I asked, "what are these "fish"? She responded that they were from the fifth dimension, the world of spirit. Then they asked me "where have you been this whole time"? With their eyes upon me, the entire room quieted. I was confused by their question, not knowing what they may have meant. I quickly learned that it wasn't where I lived that was in question; it was something else. I was asked to go see the princess of their tribe but I never found the time.

About two years prior to this incident; we traveled to Arizona on vacation. We walked into the location of our original stock exchange which had been in Bisbee, Arizona. The exchange has now been converted into a dimly lit bar. In the very back of this large room were glass display cases and a seated, Native American male wearing a crisp, white, linen shirt. His cases were filled with crystals of various shapes and sizes but all were the white/clear type. He told me that they were priceless and I couldn't buy one however, after we finished our talk, he immediately knew the crystal I wanted and let me pick it out from a special box he kept under the counter. During our conversation, he expressed that he was deeply concerned about microwaves. He had seen many things and after seeing these things he was left with no choice but to conclude that microwaves were killing the world of spirit. It just so happened that when we had our satellite dish installed the fifth-dimensional "fish" left our premises. It made me wonder what the purpose(s) was for giving us this and other technologies e.g. 5G and I became as concerned as he was.

Every April for the first three years I heard a tree knock after I had gone outside once stepping out onto the snow. The knock would always come from where the altar used to be, a densely forested spot. The snow was up to my hips so walking there was out of the question. If only one person came out of the house then, consequently, there would be only one knock.

As time passed, I was getting closer to leaving the area for good. I went outside just prior to dusk when there was still plenty of light. I took in the last of the day's warmth watching the sun's rays turn the earth a glittering, golden hue. Feeling at peace a thought entered my mind… "would you be afraid if you saw Bigfoot". I mentally said "no"; after all, after what I've been through why should this rattle me. I saw it out of my slightly peripheral vision 40° to my left. It was walking about 85 feet from me for a distance of approximately 45 feet on the opposite side of our fence toward where the altar used to be. It didn't turn its head to face me, was dark grey in color, had a sagittal crest (which may have indicated an older being), had very long fingers, and a graceful curvature to its hand which didn't indicate joints. It moved along in a fluid motion. The native asked me at least three times if it was on my property. I repeated that it walked on the opposite side of our property line on the other side of our fence. At this point, he was shaking and was still extremely concerned with which side of the property line he was on. Apparently, it means something significant if it's on your property. He literally backed up form me while still talking and said "you wonder why all of this is happening to you; it is because you live in one of the most "holy" of places" but to me what he said meant that I lived in a place where all hell breaks loose".

A few years passed with no shortage of paranormal activity. I walked over to our bedroom window gazing past my garden down the gentle slope beyond and saw, rolling upon the ground, a black mist coming in from the South. I've walked down a lot of paths trying to solve what has been going on and on one of them I read that the Djinn like to be hidden and appear to be dark mists, smoke, or a dark fog.

> *Black-robed humanoids, often called demons, appeared after waves of UFO activity and were seen in areas hit by the plague in Europe that killed twenty-five million people.*

A couple of months beforehand I heard the pastor, a neighbor of ours, stating that many people in the area had become possessed. He and a few others were trying to exorcise them. Crimes against children and murders were being committed. By this time little was strange to me and there is even less now that I've seen the black mist rolling upon the ground.

> *Over the past few years in Italy there have been unsettling and skyrocketing demands for exorcisms. On a Vatican Radio interview, Benigno Palilla detailed a week-long event scheduled to be held on April, 2018. At the time*

it was estimated that one half of one million cases of possession had been reported. As if this finding isn't distressing enough even though not all of these cases are genuinely connected to actual possessions, a jaw-dropping number of exorcisms indicate that some sort of sinister surge occurring.

Are we noticing increased evil in the world or are we becoming aware of its presence as it blatantly manifests, emigrating itself into our lives seemingly unhindered by any known means?

Palilla pointed out that the spike may be due to Italy's mystics however Italy has always had mystics. What of the rest of the "like" phenomena that is occurring simultaneously throughout the world? Palilla warned that partaking in such practices and or procedures have opened up portholes e.g. Cern, ritual/religious practices or, by other means. He claimed that opening these intended and deliberately placed barriers has opened the door to "the devil" and will eventually lead to the circumstance of <u>mass</u> possession.

Google has signed an agreement to join Cern Openlab. Together they will work to explore the possibilities for joint research and development projects in cloud, machine, and quantum computing. Their partnership was written about in the Christian Journal. Its headline read: Creation of the D-Wave Quantum Artificial Intelligence is the "altar of an alien god". Science is bringing in the antichrist system. The article went on to say that with CIA funding, the computer is becoming so powerful that it is described as "tapping into the fundamental fabric of reality; being near one is like" standing at the altar of an alien God".

Founder of the D-Wave, Geordie Rose, made light of his being able to access other dimensions and warned that demons are coming when he compared artificial intelligence to aliens. He also said there's a 25% chance that within 13 years superintelligence will take over. He compared AI with aliens, the demons (the old gods) that will be coming. Intel has a forty-nine-cubit-quantum computing chip; a Maltese Cross is part of its design and it is in its center. This same cross is depicted in Mesopotamian texts just as it is on Celine Dion's childrens', asexual clothing line. It exalts the twelfth planet's (planet X where the alleged Annunaki live) radiance. A cylinder seal found at Nippur depicted a group of plowmen looking up with awe at the twelfth planet which was illustrated as the cross and was visible in the skies.

After two years of extensive upgrades, the Large Hadron Collider warmed up for another round of experiments. Among its curiosities, Czerniski and her colleagues needed to sort out an artifact in the data. When it recreated in three-dimensions, it appeared to be a ghostly outline of a dolphin. At first, they thought it was merely the computer's desktop wallpaper bleeding through a transparent window. After they confirmed the terminal's settings, they dove deeper into the data. Their subsequent analysis suggested the apparition was real; it was registering a five sigma.

In another one of Cern's orchestrated collisions (colliding particles together) they saw apparitions that didn't fit into any of their models. They were unable to deny their reality. Something scary and unexplainable was going on. If a thing isn't explainable and doesn't seem to fit into a scientist's books, he/she throws it out of the window. They have a hard time accepting the fact that there is a spirit world out there that has been created by a spirit being. Steven Hawking warned…" they are about to open Pandora's box. Once that box has been opened what comes out of the box cannot be put back". Geordie Rose, founder of the D-Wave summoned demons through a porthole that was created by Cern. It is said that currently they are building a Skynet and their goal is transhumanism. A Skynet by definition is an artificial neural network-based conscious group mind and an artificial general intelligence system.

Ironically or intentionally a large portion of Cern is located in the Territory of St. Genis Pouilly. In

Roman times it was called *Apolliacum*. Both the town and temple were dedicated to *Apyllon/Shiva/Horus the Destroyer*. *Cern's* logo is 666, the mark of the Beast. If in doubt, here is the URL for *Cern's* opening ceremony: *https://youtu.be/P_4yjAD9MJw* Judge for yourself as to its *maleficent intent* on humanity.

Astrophysicist Neil Degrasse has also sounded an alarm stating that if anyone wants to blow up a planet it could be done through *Cern's* attempts to recreate the "Big Bang" within a manmade structure. The structure itself has less energy holding it together than what it creates within. This frightened Stephen Hawking, an atheist. None-the-less he believes CERN could easily and suddenly, without warning, destroy our universe or create the prophesized apocalyptic events in Revelation, Chapter 6, in the Bible.

CERN is aware of the public's concerns over its experiments but it doesn't seem to matter. Dedicated to Shiva, they had a statue of the god erected outside of the Cern building while dancing Shiva's dances within the building. When the LHC was first started, some people feared the powerful accelerator would create a black hole here on Earth. It may still while they continue to increase its size and its power.

We began the process of moving out of our home to a new one. By now everything was nearly packed; we swept the floors but never found the hematite bracelet.

CHAPTER 9

A Light Beam and Bigfoot

A prominent ufologist, paranormal researcher, and author of the Mothman Prophecies, John Keel proposed that there are "window areas" throughout the world which connect our reality to parallel dimensions.

Hairy giants have a disturbing habit of turning up in areas where UFOs have been seen. One particular account tying these two together came as a result of an 1888 meeting between cattle ranchers and a group of Native Americans in Northern California. The natives described <u>three</u> "crazy bears" that descended from the sky in a small moon leaving them in the woods before taking off. Because they prefer areas with a lower anthropogenic load, the Bigfeet are usually seen in forbidden, closed off areas, or in nature reserves through which they have an ecological advantage. What humans get from a material culture the Bigfeet have obtained through the course of ecological progress.

In the Summer of 1960, numerous persons around Parsons, W. Virginia allegedly saw a gruesome eight-foot-tall being covered with shaggy hair; its two huge eyes shone red. Despite having found gigantic footprints over the years, armed possess, bloodhounds, and helicopters have chased these without success. This suggests that they must have a means of rapid transportation away from their site, a way of cloaking themselves, or of disabling us from seeing them; personally, I choose the latter.

In Iosco County a Michigan hunter having once seen a Dogman may have provided an important clue how these creatures manage to remain so elusive. The deer hunter who was also a policeman, and a marksman, settled himself among the Jack Pines around the intersection of Bissonette Road and State Highway M-65 in Western Iosco County. To the East lay Wurtsmith Air Force Base. At 2:00 P.M. he realized something was monitoring him; everything around him became cloaked in silence. He walked slowly toward his hunting group while considering what may be stalking him. Fifty yards away the brush rustled and something that looked like it was out of the movie "Predator" emerged. His report came in nearly one decade earlier before the release of the movie. The translucent shape was estimated to be seven feet tall and appeared to have been looking in his direction. The hunter described the being as being more tall than it was wide; rather than having arms or legs it appeared to have been a hole in the forest. It appeared to have been absorbing all color and light yet, at the same time, it was not a shadow. It was like a lenticular image seen on postcards. From one angle he could see the forest and from the other he could see a hole. He shot five rifle rounds and three six-round speed loaders from his pistol directly at the shape to no effect at which time he threw his rifle to the ground and fled.

Another peak period for UFO activity coincided with a major outbreak of alleged monsters across the country in 1966. In one particular instance thumping was heard on the back of a car. A "hairy-man" was reported to be over six feet tall, had huge shoulders, was covered with hair, and its head was either pulled down onto its shoulders or that it didn't have a head at all. Reports of being headless or neckless are similar to the descriptions of Mothman in many of its sightings. When Dogs track the Bigfeet they lose their scent. This may be accomplished by a rapid ascent, dimensional shift, or perhaps an enzyme. People are continuing to report seeing these beings and or the evidence they have left behind.

On September second, 2013, my husband and I drove 150 miles to the nearest town to run errands and to visit a friend of mine. While at his work my enthused friend, Eugene, told us about an encounter he had hours before in the nearby woods. He and his son recorded an exceptionally long Bigfoot call. He had previous recordings of what he believed to be this being and has sought after it for over 35 years since his first sighting as I recall. He got in around 1:00 in the morning the day we came to see him; he played his recording for us. The area the recording took place in was studded with lay-lines. My husband and I finished up our business and were on our way home traveling on West Side Road past the Rocky Point juncture. Driving his truck, my husband said: "what the hell is that?" I hadn't a clue and asked that we pull over immediately. The truck slid a bit on the shoulder; its wheels spun on the loose rock until we were finally able to get out kicking the doors open with our cameras in hand. What we saw looked like a swarm of insects traveling in a stream over seven miles long at dusk. I turned around 180 degrees while telling my husband that something was there and I was going to photograph it. When I got home, I brought my pictures up on the computer. I saw that I had photographed a beam coming down to the forest floor that had orbs (plausible pulses) traveling within it.

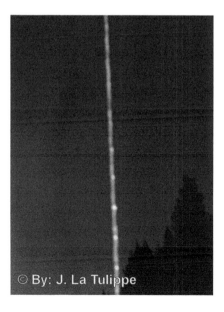

© By: J. La Tulippe

This beam was photographed in the same area that the Bigfoot call was recorded. All-in-all I took three photographs. In the first photo (S.W) there was one light in the sky and in the second there were two more making a total of <u>three</u> that were hoovering, appearing as if to draw attention (a blind) from the main event, the beam. The picture of the beam with the orbs traveling in it was surrounded by what we believed were mosquitoes.

> *A technician from St. Petersburg walked into an area recalling becoming suddenly very disoriented even though he knew the area quite well, yet, he kept walking in circles. A cognition came over him that a giant disk had descended. Once seeing the disc, he was able to walk further. He came to a clearing and noticed a giant, silver-furred man over 9' tall in the distance disappearing behind the trees. The site couldn't be investigated until later that year. It was found that the bark had been torn off some of the trees at a height of 9' from which it was learned that insects had been eaten.*

At another time, in this same area, I lost approximately 23 minutes of time while driving. Descending the mountain's steep grade and hairpin turns were treacherous. If I hadn't downshifted, my not going over the cliff wouldn't have been an option. After passing Fish Lake, nearing the sign indicating a "grade", I saw some sort of a whitish substance in the air. When I entered it, I didn't seem to notice it any longer. I traveled along a bit noticing that the scenery kept repeating itself. All-in-all there were roughly four of these scenes that repeated themselves until I finally found myself down the mountain. Having arrived 23 minutes ahead of schedule I would have to have been traveling at an impossible, life-ending speed which couldn't have been the case.

Meanwhile back at the ranch, near the middle of the night, we had repeated incidences of heavy-handed, hand-slapping on the S.E. wall of our bedroom and found that the stems on our mist sprinkler system were unscrewed and were laid neatly beside where they had been taken off. One day, I found a single barefoot footprint (outside of human dimensions) leading toward the lot next door where the alter had been and coincidentally or not…another sprinkler stem had been unscrewed near the footprint. Within the blink of an eye, the winds came up erasing the print from the soft, silica soil as if it had never been there.

CHAPTER 10

Bigfoot Indicators in Association with a UFO

On June 11, 2013, I awoke at 11:03 P.M. due to an intense and long-lingering feeling of arousal. I had no related dreams so I knew its cause had to have been externally initiated in order to have me generate a specific frequency. I believe that the orange orb's purpose was to collect that frequency.

Cautiously, I arose looking around as I walked through the house making my way toward the back, glass door. Hoovering soundlessly, nearly 150' away and 20' off the ground was a 15' wide orange orb. Two sections in the positions of two o'clock and the other at 7 o'clock were a brighter orange than the rest of the orb. The edges of its sections/wedges were jagged but each of the two edges mirrored the first edge of its section. I walked out to the site two weeks later with my metal detector. The detector didn't indicate anything of interest but the surrounding air was filled with static electricity and made the hair on my arms stand up on end.

Living in the woods at the time I became familiar with its sounds. On June 27, 2013, I awoke to something calling out at evenly spaced intervals and noticed they had a faint human quality to them. Hearing these calls, I woke my husband and asked if he heard anything. He said he never heard anything like it and that it sounded really, really scary. Continuing our conversation, we found we were unable to move with the exceptions of lifting our heads off of our pillow and were able to lift our hands off the mattress so far as our wrists would allow while we continued to listen. Because we were carrying on a full conversation, we were aware that we were not experiencing sleep paralysis. Each call was preceded with a strong, heavy, breathy, rasp. It felt as though I was laying on the left side of its chest; its vocalization was loudest behind my right ear.

In another time in Russia, scientists used female ape pheromones and found that three Bigfeet came near their encampment. The Bigfeet responded with heavy breathing and grunts leaving their memorable footprints behind. The scientists experienced terror and panic even though they were strong and well-armed.

At the time of a Russian, Bigfoot research and expedition project, it was thought that this creature could do anything that Homos archetypal Homosapiens' ancestors and modern humans could do in their proverbial stage of evolution. I believe the Bigfeet are at the state where we'd return to if we were to reboot. From experiencing and reading what I have, they have the qualities that were given to us in the past through our ancient DNA. The traits that were found to be most admired included telepathic communication, the ability to influence people (filling them with fear and, at times, just short of paralysis), the ability to find a lost person, the ability to remote view, and etc. Currently, these traits are all intentionally being bred out of the modern human. It seems as though they are being culled and are being passed onto another group or a race and will be used for the purposes of communicating with interdimensional beings and flying craft.

A report was published in 1990 that took place in Mongolia. It was written up in a Russian Digest regarding Russian soldiers who fought against the Japanese Imperial Army. Two corpses were found lying in the sand and were considered to be the size of an average human. They were thought to have been anthropoid apes that were covered with uneven, reddish/brownish hair.

Their hands were disproportional in relation to their body's size. They had exceptionally long fingers (like that I've publicly reported in my first sighting). The soldiers reported seeing their silhouettes close to dawn. They were walking slowly along the apex of the sandhill. Both beings didn't heed their halt warnings so the sentry shot them both. An old Mongol said, "what the sentry shot were two wild-men that lived in the areas' mountains".

In 1941 a man was captured in the Caucus Mountains. A doctor examined him and found that the subject was human in all of his forms with the exception that his head, chest, and shoulders were covered with thick, dark, brown hair. He was large, had broad shoulders, and was quite muscular. He would not eat or drink in captivity and sweated profusely. Its gaze was obscure and empty as though his examiners were looking into an empty soulless vessel.

I went outside and saw a single barefoot, footprint on the side of the house where our headboard would have been nearly aligned. Researchers have often found a single print and, as per usual on these occasions, it has been the left one. They have also stated that it is the left print that is found before the creature disappears into another dimension. I could barely leave a .25-inch impression in the same soil conditions (next to the suspected Bigfoot print). The print I found was 2.5 inches deep. Roughly 75 feet away we had a chicken coop with an attached enclosed chicken yard. The very top of the enclosure, for its entire length, was matted with grey hair/fur. Shortly thereafter an un unpredicted, heavy rain occurred, washing away any traces of evidence.

A couple of days afterward, about three through five feet from the footprint, I found an eyedropper. If you were familiar with the terrain and knowing how remote our neighbors were, the likelihood of this happening might be something like one in one million let alone having been found by a footprint outside of a human's dimensions.

As a result of reporting this incident I got nothing but grief; those that were supposed to investigate the incident refused to.

Frustrated, I started to get some tools that would help me render supporting proof.

> *I was granted permission to ghost-hunt the Goldfield hotel by its proprietor at the time, Virginia Ridgeway. Virginia allowed me to use her Ovilius which was given to her by its creator as a personal gift. We heard amazing things through it and were able to go into areas of the hotel she was not, due to her age. The Ovilius relayed credible information regarding the crime that recently occurred there that was later reported to the police. Through my unusual abilities I was able to corroborate the information gathered from the hotel's mailbox and from a gravesite disclosing much more information to Virginia. Virginia, once hearing what we reported, verified what we found. All of the activity made for a memorable day. Having had a reliable and proven experience with this instrument, this is one of the tools I decided to attain having had such great success with it.*

My Ovilius, with its built-in E.M. meter, finally arrived. It was a newer model than I previously used with the added advantage of showing the words it relaying into text. I took it out of the box and, at first, it spouted nonsensical gibberish. I knew purchasing this was a gamble but just having it for the E.M. meter would have been appreciated. I let it rest before taking it in hand again. I pointed it to the back window and it described our forested lot perfectly. My husband said, "let me see that". He pointed it at me and it said: "French, female". Testing it further, he wasn't disappointed. I took it back and it spoke while I walked. I went into the closet and it told me it was dark in there. I went out into the back of the house. From the back of the house it described the ground that I was walking on along with so many other features after I asked it tell me anything relevant.

CHAPTER 11

Seeing Through the Veil

I met a new friend at a UFO symposium through a cryptid researcher, an associate of mine. This was the first time I was able to meet the researcher in person. I found out that my new friend was a medium and has worked through a paranormal society in Pennsylvania.

I'll call the cryptid researcher Sal. Sal drew my attention to a photograph that was taken back in the woods five miles off of a main road in West Virginia.

> *For your consideration, before I go on with this story I think I should point out an intriguing occurrence has been found when matter is cooled to near absolute zero. The process is called Supersolidity. Supersolidity occurs when a crystalline structure and a frictionless flow occur together.*
>
> *There are three states of matter that are encountered on a daily basis whether a thing may be a solid, gas, or a liquid. It's difficult to imagine substances simultaneously exhibiting properties of two states of matter yet, in quantum physics, matter can display behaviors that seem to be mutually exclusive. Supersolidity is <u>one example of this paradoxical state</u>. Now that I've written this I can go on with the rest of my story.*

There was a mound in the photograph Sal had produced which he referred to as a grave and on top of what he referred to as a grave was what looked like a cave's entrance. Of course, none of this was seen with the human eye at the time but the camera's I.R. picked it up. The top and sides of the cave's entrance looked tunnel-shaped and were covered in something that looked like white chiffon which was tattered at its bottom. Looking at the photo, I was stunned.

In our conversation, I told him I was gifted like my new friend was but the gifts bestowed upon me were a little different because I worked primarily detecting and literally decoding energy. The saying goes: "talk is cheap" so Sal put me to the test.

He handed me his smartphone showing me the picture that was taken. He asked what I thought of it; I responded "companion". He bent down looking directly into my eyes and said "what"? I repeated my answer. As he stared at me, I felt that I was being scrutinized having recollected that he served in law enforcement. His expected response took longer than I anticipated. Finally, he said, "did you say companion?" I said "I did" then he asked how I got that. I told him that when I mentally asked the question the response came back "companion". He said, "there's another one". I asked "another what?" He said there is another mound. By this time, he stepped back from me with his mouth gaping. Still, I was happy that I gave him a correct answer but I could tell he still finds difficulty in comprehending an ability beyond the acknowledged five senses. I called him later regarding the picture that we previously discussed telling him what was in the ground beneath the recently created mound. I also told him that the symbolism found there was pagan and it was not Native American. He said that he had spoken to the Native Americans in the area and what I told him corroborated with what they told him.

I told him that this was all I could come up with for now but I would attempt to meditate on it further to see what else I could get. A few weeks later my home quieted down and I found the peace I needed. Someone recently has broken into my home and took a journal I was recording the words I received while meditating so I will do my best to recall what happened.

I called Sal back and told him that the mist/chiffon was similar to what I had seen on a T.V. show that was described as an electric fog whereupon a plane, once flying into this mist, flew to an unplanned location that had a strange effect on the plane's instruments. The plane traveled a great distance far afield from the pilot's intended route. It was found to have an excess of fuel that it shouldn't have had due to the distance it traveled. It would have been impossible to have reached its location in the time it traveled. This fog seems to have or accompany the ability to transport objects amending their timeframe. Then I received the word "mother". I inherently knew that mother in this case meant overseer, someone that controls, guides, and protects. I also received another word, one that I can't currently recall; it was in my stolen journal. The word, because I looked it up at the time, turned out to be a village in East Africa. Further research indicated that it was the only area that has a clicking language. The clicking language is what Bigfoot is reported to use. As a result, I reported to Sal that he did indeed find a Bigfoot area and that the Bigfeet being there or not, or, the ability to see them or not, was regulated by an overseer "mother" in this case. He then told me about one other picture that was taken.

The other men involved whose trailcam it was where the photograph was taken from were able to take another picture of the mound but this time the mound had a domed glowing red object on top of it. I have a pretty good idea what was going on there at the time. Those that initially took the pictures with the trailcam were coveting the pictures and refused to show them to anyone else other than Sal. By this time they didn't even want to show more of them to him. Perhaps this was because Sal had been telling them what I thought/knew. Sal told me that I had been 100% correct all of the four times that I gave him information from my remote location across the country. He's not one to sit idly by and not fact check. The men taking the pictures have been trying to acquire as much knowledge from Sal as possible but have continued to refuse to share their knowledge with him.

For several weeks in September, 1989, two hundred miles South of Moscow, unidentified lights were seen over the city. On the 27th it was reported that a spacecraft was seen landing in a public park whereupon three, 9-foot-tall figures emerged. Scientists studied the site and some military gathered samples which were posted in the International Press. The article was endorsed by the Soviet News Agency. The figures drawn by the school children witnessing the event were Bigfoot looking. Some of their drawings showed a cone-shaped head, others reported seeing their body but not their head, while others reported a sudden disappearance. As stated by the adults e.g. school teachers, scientists, and etc. was that giant-like beings exited their craft to do research. The squeaking sounds heard were thought to have been a drill. A large amount of witness corroborated with one another.

CHAPTER 12

If a Circle had a Beginning

I've come across some pretty interesting things in my lifetime; one was the story about the Pre-Endomite kings. The text I read stated that they never had a beginning but instead it suggested that they always were as was the condition to whom many refer to as God. God wanted these kings to do as He commanded. They refused and because of this it is alleged that Jesus was created; God knew that Jesus would never disobey Him. The text continued to say that these kings descended to earth.

A crystal is known to have the ability to open portholes. When Lucifer was cast out from heaven, he was said to have worn a large crystal around his neck. Did Lucifer use it for this purpose? Did he escape his intended outcome by opening up a porthole allowing him to descend to Earth where he and his would be perceived as the gods? The Poseidon religion was born out of Atlantis; Atlantis is the place where the gods came down.

It has been written that the Pre-Endomites, Illuminati, the fallen angels, and or perhaps those with elongated skulls felt that their technology gave them the right to rule the world and that they and they alone were worthy. In their eyes it is the humans, the Adam (man) that were wicked. They think humans are fools and have no legitimate claim to the earth. Simply put, Neanderthal Man is said to have been the test. In the Candelabra Theory he is what is sometimes called a Pre-Adamite however, in the Noah's Ark Theory the Neanderthal is a Co-Adamite. These opinions have been around for a surprisingly long time. Co-Adamism is the term used when true men existed contemporaneously with Adam who were not descended from him. Co-Adamism is a necessary corollary of polygenism.

A DNA analysis was done on the elongated Paracas skulls. The results were published on March 4, 2018, in Alien/Earth/Science/UFO/Unexplained. The analysis showed that they could have come from an entirely new species outside of the known evolutionary tree. The sample proved itself to be unlike any known human DNA. A question posed regarding the skull analysis was: why did it take so long getting to this analysis? One thought was that the elongated skulls were those of the Pre-Adamite ancestors which we now call the Illuminati, synonymous with the New World Order.

Cloning facilities enabled the Pre-Endomites to multiply throughout the earth. One of their creations, the giants, cannibalized humans. It was suspected that this was so because the food produced couldn't keep up with what was needed to maintain their bodies' mass however this is likely too simplistic of an explanation, instead, the consumption of man may allude to the taking of man's soul into themselves.

"In the June 8, 1991 issue of Science News, there was an article on Father O'Connell's complaint. The article written by Bruce Bower regarded the "Neanderthal's Disappearing Act,". It was an exceedingly technical discussion on the hybridization or the non-hybridization of Neanderthal Man.

Milford Wolpoff of the University of Michigan contended that there is a regional continuity in Europe evidenced by the Neanderthals having appeared on the scene 100,000 years ago. They are on the direct ancestral line of modern humans. The theory claims that there is no single Adam nor an Eve but instead, there are thousands of them from whom we've descended known as polygenism (many first parents, as opposed to monogenism, a single pair). Fr. Teilhard de Chardin, said: "the first man is and can only be a crowd. Mans' infancy is made up of thousands and thousands of years" despite that Cann et al. say that we are all descended from a single woman. They still haven't really espoused monogenism, since they maintain that there were true men before and after "mitochondrial Eve" who were not descended from her.

Neanderthals may have constituted a separate species (H. neandertalensis). Other evidence of clear biological separation of Neanderthals and moderns is provided by the persistence of the two populations separate identities over a long period. The Kebara Neanderthal may have lived 40,000 years after the two populations, yet this specimen shows no sign of hybridization with modern humans—in fact, they show no features that might be ascribed to previous hybridizations with Neanderthals."

Early man's way of thinking is hypothesized to have been exceedingly modern and complex. In this early culture, real and symbolic words were intertwined. There was a continuity and a sequence in man's ritual and ceremonial relationship to that world. Art, image, and notation were their means to express a complex reality.

Neanderthal Man is still misrepresented in illustrations and statuary in museums as having a short neck with the head bent forward. Unlike those depictions, it has become clear from their skeletons that the spinal column was perfectly normal, and their head is fitted on straight and was not at an angle, as in the case of apes.

On the cover of the October 1988 issue of National Geographic, a photograph depicted a small bust carved in ivory of a Neanderthal Man found near Dolni Vestonice, Czechoslovakia near Brno (a Neanderthal site). The carving was examined under a microscope and was found to be authentic. The carving was that of a Neanderthal with the suborbital ridge, and etc. In no *way did it look ape-like. It was clearly that of a rugged, but handsome, human being.*

The giants, having eaten humans (taking mans' soul into themselves, begged God for His forgiveness. God denied them forgiveness seeing that their vessel/body <u>was not worthy of housing the spirit</u> and as such, Noah's flood was brought about in an attempt to purge them from the earth attempting to start fresh so that a new and worthy body could be created.

It has been written before they became the Illuminati the survivors from the suspected turmoil on Mars built a civilization in the Sahara Desert. Some of the Endomites from Europe and Asia are said to have survived, migrated to Egypt, and became Pharaoh. What happened in Atlantis was their third world destruction event as described in the book "Edgar Cayce on Atlantis". They eventually setup kingdoms throughout the world.

According to an ancient papyrus 3,500 years ago, during the reign of King Tutmosis III, Egypt was invaded by spherical UFOs for several days. They were described as circles of fire. In the temple of Hathor what may be considered images of alien beings were images of the heads of Reptilians having the bodies of what looks like a Bigfoot that were found on its walls in Dendera, Egypt. Other images on the walls were Reptilian-humanoid beings along-side of the Pharaohs and that of bird-headed beings. There were also images of strange, giant lightbulbs that may have plausibly been some sort of a plasma beam weapon. The filament inside of the bulb looked like a sake/Reptilian. This may have been a pictorial message that alien plasma technology was given to the upper strata of their society for their exclusive use by the serpent/Reptilian race of alien beings.

It was from Sumer that the white-skinned people from the Caucasus Mountains N.E. of the Nile River Delta spread blood rituals and magick through the rest of the world. Zachariah Sitchin and John Marco Allegro studied ancient Sumerian clay tablets discovered at Nineveh in the 1800s. The tablets revealed that the Sumerian empire was formed by invading aliens called the Annunaki. Summa's original name was Ki.En.Gir (gia) (land of the king with blazing rockets). The Zoroastrian, Hindu, and Judaic religions all began in the Sumerian Empire.

The Zomer is the worst of all Jewish cults. It is a secret organization based in Turkey. They believed the Messiah would come if all people were pure evil or if they were solely good. Their belief gave rise to incredible immorality and insidious evil deeds. They twisted the Torah around believing it was easier to be evil than it was to be good. They believed that there was a given amount of evil as well as good in the universe. By committing continuous, maleficent crimes against themselves and humanity they believed that the evil energy in the Universe would finally be used up, the universe would collapse, and the Messiah would come. The founder of the cult converted to Islam and he was believed to have been God. They spread throughout Europe taking over entire communities having made them Satanic and are intent on destroying the bible. There is a connection from this cult to the Illuminati. Essentially what they are saying is that the entire world has to be reduced to pure evil so that God will come.

*In a radio interview, Gary Parker said he would like to restore the Great Pyramid and the Sphinx somewhat. Egypt has 284 billion dollars of debt; he thought it would be good for their economy. In addition, he wanted to include a twenty-four-hour surveillance on the pyramid through its restorative process. He contacted Elon Musk and Sir Richard Branson to see if they would be interested in the project; both responded positively. Gary downloaded a couple of images from the space station (the international space station's number is **ISS032-E-009123**) clicked on Nasa Pyramids Giza, Egypt, then he clicked on the full-size image of the Sphinx and Great Pyramid which enabled him to contemplate where the needed personnel should be placed.*

The pictures from the space station had been taken by an astronaut. After downloading one of the photos Gary zoomed in on the Great Pyramid. Having zoomed in he saw letters on the ground in what looked like Aramaic or Hebrew. He wrote the letters down and took a picture of them with his phone, e-mailed them to a couple of Judaic and Aramaic scholars, and to a couple of Egyptologists then to the folks that worked on the Dead Sea Scrolls asking if the letters said anything. The letters on the North side of the Great Pyramid translated into "I am who I am creator of all things". In the near proximity, he found more lettering by a smaller pyramid that was translated by Dr. Edward Wright, Director at Arizona Center for Judaic Studies into "God and the Lord of the Underworld".

On the Egyptian coronet the vulture was seen at times side-by-side with the serpent on its bottom half. The bottom portion of the coronet represented lower Egypt in the North, where the pyramids are in the river delta area. The rivers in this area form a trident and the pyramids themselves are in the pattern of Orion the "hunter". For those of you who haven't thought about is this way, a hunter is a predator. The trident's formation may be a symbol representing the inverted trinity which conveys an infernal meaning ascribed to the number three. The lower portion of their coronet that had the Reptilian on it is also associated with demonic powers and a dark religion that was dominant in the area at the time.

Dr. Wright also found a date; the date was July 26, 2022. He speculated that it may be the date this god is supposed to return to the city of David in Jerusalem. The date's numerical value is three and again this is a reference to the infernal trinity. A couple of the Judaic and Aramaic scholars got back to Gary and said the lettering was almost as tall as the pyramid itself.

Neanderthal Man is clearly Homo Sapiens, Sapiens and is not a separate species. Homo Sapiens Neandertalensis may have been hybridized or may have replaced other races of men. Father

O'Connell speculated that he may have been from the race of Cain which perished in the deluge and that the disputed evidence of hybridization between Neanderthals and Cro-Magnons in Israel, might be the result of intermarriages between the race of Seth and the race of Cain which is mentioned in Genesis 6:2.

Many have heard the story of Adam and Eve however I imagine there is only a small percentage of those that have heard why it is that a woman that was chosen from a higher source as Adam's mate was made to appear as though she committed an offense against God and humankind.

We have to first consider what side of the fence this god/God spoken of is on. I propose that the story of Adam and Eve is not a creation story but it is rather an amendment story/hybridization story in our ongoing developmental process.

Many believe that a clear connection exists between the Anunnaki and representations of Reptilian beings here on Earth. Let us say that we've subscribed to the story that Adam and Eve are in The Garden of Paradise and let us say that Satan presented himself to them in Reptilian form and that he was given dominion over all of the earth in the all too familiar story of Adam and Eve.

What if everything we have been taught is wrong? What if the serpent never tempted Eve? Historical accounts tell us of a race of Reptilian beings who descended from the heavens, participated in creating humankind, taught the sciences, imparted forbidden knowledge, imposed social order, breed with us, watch over our development, and exercise mind-control over human captives while performing medical procedures on us.

> *Months ago, I met a woman in a supervisory position in the UFO field that had an opportunity to travel onto the Western Pacific sea for eighteen years. During her voyage, she saw Reptilian statues on many of the islands. At times they were shown in a family unit. She has taken many pictures of them omitting 1,000 of the photos from her report because she only wanted the best included. She believes that in some way we have descended from them.*

I remember seeing what is called a "cosmic egg" which is a very large representation of an egg in stone. I first saw it on an informative television channel and of course, they have been found in other places throughout the world. The egg had a representation of a DNA strand on the top of it in relief. This is a two-stranded model and although I have seen repeatedly that this is what ours looks like, what you have been told is false! Further reading in this text will describe our DNA strand more fully. The point I want to make is that what looks like a DNA strand associated with us humans is seen on this egg. Humans have life births but Reptilians, for the most part, lay eggs.

In their illustrations, the Sumerians left behind images of Enki which were Reptilian in appearance. The legend inferred that Enki possessed a highly advanced technology that included the capability of genetically altering an indigenous species using a mysterious process having created a clay-like substance binding upon it the "image of the gods". This account is similar to what has been relayed in the creation story of Adam having been created from clay. This excerpt about Enki was written much earlier than the story of Adam's creation. What is interpreted by this is that Enki used Anunnaki genes to create a hybrid species. It also implies that some early humans may have been Reptilian in their appearance.

An account of a Sumerian King was inscribed onto clay tablets 240,000 years ago. This was the story of the god Anu, the chief god of an extraterrestrial race called the Anunnaki and that of his two sons Enki and Enlil. In 1945, in a small town in Egypt, a clay jar was found bearing ancient scrolls similar to the Dead Sea Scrolls known as the Nag Hammadi Texts. The texts spoke of the human creation story. The bodies of Adam and Eve were described as being overlaid with a <u>horny skin</u>, and were like a luminescent garment as bright as daylight.

An archeologist I heard talked about his interviewing Iraqi Bedouins. When they disclosed their verbal history, they relayed that they are the descendants of the Reptilians. I recently purchased this piece of jewelry seen below from a Sumerian who was all too familiar with their verbal lore/history; who better to make this piece than a Sumerian/Iraqi? The stone it carries in its mouth is flint suggesting what comes out of its mouth spews fire's destruction.

Carl Sagan pointed out that in the core of our brain lies our Reptilian past which is called the R-complex. It is that part of the brain performing aggressive, ritual, and territorial behaviors, and the establishment of social hierarchies. It is essentially a reflex action.

The middle layer, the limbic system, is thought to generate love, hate, compassion, and sentimentality. These are the characteristics that are believed to be strictly mammalian.

Thinking back… our creator wanted us to have nothing to do with the Tree of Knowledge of Good and Evil. However, in the book of Genesis, The Tree of Knowledge of Good and Evil may really have been a metaphor for our neocortex. The neocortex is responsible for reasoning and deliberation, a place where we know the difference between good and evil.

I find it interesting that the female embodies the act of creation yet the church has demonized her. We have to ask ourselves is it because she accepted having a neocortex the thought of which will put everything into question.

If genetic engineering was in fact used in the metaphor of a Garden of Eden (which has often been referred to as a lab) having an awareness of good and evil via the neocortex (which was chosen by Eve) enabled her to pass this genetic attribute onto her children.

Having been amended, through Eve's choice and use of her free will, humanity became more mammalian and less Reptilian and, as a consequence, "man" fell out of grace with his creator, the Reptilian.

Historical accounts of Reptilians or their hybridizing are found among the Romans, Greeks, Chinese, Galician folklore, Portuguese, India, Peru, Islamic, Hindu, Hopi, and in Chili. There are likely a host of others; some are seen below.

- Boreas (Aqualon to the Romans): the Greek god of the cold North wind was described by Pausanias as a winged man, sometimes with serpents instead of feet.[1]
- Cecrops I: the mythical first King of Athens was half man and half snake.
- Dragon Kings: creatures from Chinese mythology were sometimes depicted as Reptilian humanoids.
- Some Djinn in Islamic mythology are described as alternating between human and serpentine forms.
- Echidna, the wife of Typhon in Greek mythology, was half woman and half snake.
- Fu Xi: serpentine founding figure from Chinese mythology.
- Glycon: a snake god who had the head of a man.
- The Gorgons: Sisters in Greek mythology had serpents for hair.
- The Lamia: a child-devouring female demon from Greek mythology was depicted as half woman and half serpent.
- Nāga (Devanagari: नाग): Reptilian beings (king cobras) from Hindu mythology[2] were said to live underground and interact with human beings on the surface.
- Ningizzida, Lord of the Tree of Life was mentioned in the Epic of Gilgamesh and linked to the water serpent constellation Hydra.
- Nüwa: serpentine founding figure from Chinese mythology
- Serpent: an entity from the Genesis creation narrative occasionally depicted with legs, and sometimes identified

with Satan, though its representations have been both male and female.[3]

- <u>Shenlong</u>: a Chinese dragon thunder god, depicted with a human head and a dragon's body
- Sobek: Ancient Egyptian crocodile-headed god
- Suppon No Yurei: A turtle-headed human ghost from Japanese mythology and folklore
- Tlaloc: Aztec god depicted as a man with snake fangs
- Typhon, the "father of all monsters" in Greek mythology, had a hundred snake-heads in Hesiod,[4] or else was a man from the waist up, and a mass of seething vipers from his waist down.
- <u>Wadjet</u> pre-dynastic snake goddess of Lower Egypt, was sometimes depicted as half snake and half woman
- <u>Zahhak</u>, a figure from Zoroastrian mythology who, in Ferdowsi's epic Shahnameh, grows a serpent on either shoulder

At a local level in the U.S., we have the Lizard Man of Scape Ore Swamp in South Carolina and Jake the Alligator Man in Washington.

Additional accounts of Reptilians not only include incredible knowledge they have imparted but also include their numerous heinous acts which were the likely outcome from the R-Complex. One example is the story of Lamia, **Queen of Libya,** *who became a* <u>child-murdering</u> *monster feared for her malevolence depicted as being covered in scales. Egyptian hieroglyphs are studded with images of hybrid Reptilians.*

"In Teilhard's theory, original sin cannot be localized in a historical chain of events. Rather it is a global modality of evolution... Strictly speaking, there is no Adam. In his view, Adam is a symbol epitomizing that all men are born fallen, that all are marked by original sin the instant they become members of mankind. But men are not born in sin because of some aboriginal sin of a primitive Adam. Men are born in original sin because this is the law of the universe, the cosmic condition of a world in evolution."

Have the fallen been included in (the supernal) man? Once leaving their original form they had been abolished until mans' representation came forth, the representation of Adam. When the form of Adam was configurated, they all exist having been restored in this condition. The acknowledgment of their continued existence is contingent on mankind's manipulation and or mans' intended distractions rendering them unconscious through the use of programming, media, politics, resource control, pharmaceuticals, and other means.

CHAPTER 13

Entering a Garden

Here is the garden you were intended to walk in. Its grass is lush and cool under your feet. It's a place where you feel that you could spend eternity languishing in its splendor on what is referred to as the "blue marble". There are two trees in this, your garden, from where much of your meal was taken and prepared for you. <u>They</u> took it from the tree <u>they</u> chose without your questioning allowing you to eat your fill set by your own pace. The meal was good and you were familiar with its fruit having been introduced to it by them slowly throughout your lives and your previous lifetimes. The tree of which I speak is called "The Tree of Good and Evil" and you eat of its fruit/technology which has been brought to you by beings not of this earth.

Whosoever looks for the paths that lead beyond this world of the senses will soon learn to understand that human life only gains in worth and significance through insight into another world. People will be prone to demand that irrefutable proofs are to be given for what has been stated but they do not realize that in doing so they fall victim to a misconception. Unconsciously, they won't demand the proofs lying within the things themselves, but only to those that they personally are willing to recognize or are in a condition to recognize as man is limited to those things that he perceives through his senses. It is at this time that I'd like to remind you that man's psychic ability is being culled and bread out of us and is likely being put into another class of a being. When I was taking my biological psychology class, what Charles and I thought was actually a Grey stated that we had over 360 senses (he said the number specifically but I have forgotten the exact number. I believe it was either 364 or 365; today we only recognize five or six of them.

CHAPTER 14

The Following Generations' Legacy

Colonel Corso and his subordinates were sent on a mission to ferret out technology already in progress that was similar to what had been turned over from the Roswell crash. They sought out our universities, laboratories, and the top 25 of the fortune 400 industries in an effort to back-engineer what had been given and poured research and development contracts into those that they chose. For example, as a result of gathered technologies, if a transistor or an integrated circuit was already being worked on, the integrated circuit turned into "the supercomputer" within thirty years' time. Corso inquired from his general, "what are we unleashing on the world, where will it end up? What if it integrates with the human brain; are we going to create a race of monsters"? The general replied, let's hope that the people that come after us recognize the danger and, hopefully, it won't be in our lifetime.

Corsco watched the EBEs autopsies and discovered they were clones. They wore a silvery helmet with a red stone in the middle of the helmet's forehead area. This allowed them to fly their ship because they could interact with it.

The synopsis of the autopsy revealed that they had:

- two microchips (artificial intelligence) in their brain

- a brain that had four lobes
- suction cups on their fingers
- one lung
- a different lymphatic system
- five toes
- no ears
- no nose
- no mouth
- four fingers
- a stomach
- and the blood and a heart of a being that was intended to habitually fly in space.

The being asked Corsco to release him by shutting the radar down. Colonel Corsco responded, "what do you have to offer". The being replied, "A new world if you can take it". I've wondered what that meant. I didn't read the words "the new world would be given" or "earned" but I specifically read the word "taken" as if taken from something. Interesting!

On October 14th-20th in the year 2017, the 19th world festival of youths and students met from numerous different countries in Moscow and Sochi Russia. The festival's goal was to encourage the students to network with each other as friends rather than continuing to cater to the preexisting division among them.

In a closing speech, on the festival's last day, Valdimir Putin publicly warned on television that humanity is playing God with our genetic code attempting to create another human being both theoretically and practically. Not only can a gifted musician, genius, or mathematician be created but so can the ultimate soldier void of fear, compassion, and regret. Putin sees a future in which troops will be genetically modified.

Crispr is a gene editing program that is faster, cheaper, more accessible, and is allegedly more precise. It is able to cut into the genetic structure (embryo) and make its changes inserting or deleting genes. Reflecting on this statement I wonder what has been done in the past to have turned off some of our genes.

A study was published in 2017 in which researchers examined a couple of lab mice that already had been experimented on using "Crispr" in an attempt to reverse a very specific thing. Upon the completion of their examination, they reported that there were unintended procedural consequences in which some 1,600 of these unintended consequences occurred in the two mice beyond anything that Crispr had planned. Two other studies confirmed the unintended consequences of Crispr's so-called precision.

The companies using Crispr wanted to make people believe that it was safe. The developer of the program herself stated that she worries about Crisper's unintended consequences being levied onto humanity. "Anyone with a lab can gain possession of Crispr and use it", no matter their moral or mental caliber.

In the original script of "The Obsolete Man" Serling wrote of the dangers by the government viewing people as expendable once they've outgrown their usefulness to the state. The kicker is, unless they figure a way out, government through its monstrous actions will also become obsolete.

Putin wants to see stronger regulations (another thing to be ignored or breached) put upon artificial intelligence's technology before worldwide cyborg armies are activated that are stronger, faster, and more lethal than any human could ever be. It is said his disclosure may have been worse than a nuclear bomb however I already wrote about this in 2014.

In 2017 Russia disclosed that they had a bulletproof exoskeleton that would make Russian troops stronger, increase their stamina, and enable them to march further with heavier loads. This further exemplifies that we are heavily engaged in the age of transhumanism which has been brought to us through ill-gotten technology whereby man (what is said to be Gods' creation) will-be-made to mimic a machine. The opposition of mans' incorporation into a machine is expected to involve the whole of mankind in an all-encompassing battle. While still in its infancy, the developers of destruction are marketing their products under the auspices of selling the populous on convenience and personal enhancement/superiority. They're merely testing our interactions to gauge the success and function of a non-human temporary counterpart before full integration. Our true battle will be one of ethics.

Because robots can easily surmount our own abilities, people should be more than concerned; they should be scared. Our overlords have been created and when one isn't the lead dog the view of those that aren't is always the same. When a man is no longer human, he/she is no longer God's creation he/she is an "other-than", a transhuman. Once the already encroaching technology is in place, plausible safeguards and guarantees will be ignored spelling the end of all of us as we once were.

CHAPTER 15

Resetting Human Frequency

The Roman Catholic Church (Vatican Authority) is the first beast (the sea beast in Revelation 13), it is the legal Guild that set itself up in the worlds' Common Law System to which all nations owe their allegiance? The second beast is the Rothschild banking system. According to Apostle John's definition, the Pope (Vatican) and Rothschild's banking system are the ultimate antichrists.

At the collapse of the secular Roman Empire, the Vatican hired an army seizing seven European provinces of the former Roman Empire. When Pope Pius VI refused to renounce his political power, he was taken captive at which time Napoleon expelled the entire Roman Curia. The pope died during his imprisonment. Napoleon issued an order stating that a successor would not be named. Later, Napoleon wanted to be crowned Emperor in his new European kingdom and, becoming desirous of an officiating Pope, he rescinded his decision and reinstalled the position of Pope.

After Napoleon's power abdication in 1812, European nations met at the Congress of Vienna. In 1815 they drew a new map of Europe in what was named the Holy Alliance. The Alliance didn't want the Vatican to reign again as its former tyrannical self, the vicious Holy Roman Empire, nor did they want the Jesuits to be in control; consequently, they placed the Vatican's finances into the administration of a banking institute. It later came to be controlled by the Rothschilds becoming the guardians of the church's vast property ownership, and its monetary means. The Rothschilds control the key to the church's wealth.

The City of London is also known as "The Crown" and, like Washington DC, they all have an obelisk. Is this a coincidence? On February 13, 2019, the Pope and the Imam signed a "one-world religion" covenant. The greatest of concerns in this document is an ambiguous reference to God. The document uses the same term, God, to simultaneously reference Allah, claiming that there is an intentional plurality of religions and that this plurality is willed by God. I don't recall having any knowledge of God having sat in on this meeting nodding His head in agreement. Additionally, the document adheres to their claim that, if people abide by a single religion, they should be rejected. The enactment of which would allow for hundreds of different religions in which the line would be blurred between religions and cultures. According to them, they must be considered equal. Hence, we see the emergence of a one-world religion. "Sadly, this idea is not out of Pope Francis's character.

> *Not all is good alleging claims of infallible decision making. By definition, "Papal infallibility" is a Catholic Church dogma which states: in virtue of the promise of Jesus to his apostle Peter, the Pope is preserved from the possibility of making an error in the exercise of his office as shepherd and teacher of all Christians, by the virtue of his supreme apostolic authority, when he defines a doctrine".*
>
> *When I was attending Catholic school, my family subscribed to a periodical called "The Tidings". I remember my mother reading from it and through it I was told what movies I could and could not see and what historical events I could not be made aware of. Needless to say, I went a little ballistic hearing that the church didn't want me to read portions of history. Most of what I wasn't to read involved heinous acts committed by the church. I don't believe the Inquisition was one of them although, it may have been.*
>
> *During those times, women helped other women in childbirth and for doing so they were labeled witches*

and suffered persecution. Their persecution extended into their kitchens because they were the first chemists. They used herbs to medicinally treat others. At other times women were accused of being the progenitors of crop failure and were said to have attracted locusts, or that they brought on the death of an infant.

In another off-limits historical account that we weren't to know about was that of Pope Innocent XVI. He wore a large, white, opal ring signifying what I call his pseudo purity. The story that involved this Pope had to do with a large body of water that had to be crossed during the crusades. In order to arrive at their destination, the pope had his crusaders gather up approximately 300 children that were to march in front of them. It was thought that because of the children's innocence, God would part the waters in front of them enabling all to cross as the waters were reported to have been parted for Moses. Because this did not come into fruition, the pope had all of the children sold into slavery at the docks. This was called the "March of the Innocents". I'll not go into the church's concubines, land grabs, over 4,000 sexual abuse charges, wars, and articles stolen to festoon their buildings in the name of the god they worship. Because of who he represented, the pope believed this gave him the right to invade and pillage in the name of god/God.

The church took action against what they perceived were dark forces in those that they saw as ugly, disfigured, or stricken with disease. They also believed that a coven group consisted of thirteen persons. In a particular village in which a suspected witch was found, all of the females except one were murdered. The only remaining female child was spared for the sole purpose of reproduction. It didn't matter if they suspected one or two to be witches the fact of the matter was that because a coven consisted of thirteen an additional eleven or twelve had to be found one way or another. Torturing a confession out of someone always seemed to yield results. Of course, they must have forgotten all about Christ's coven in which He and his immediate/bodyguards disciples made a total

128

of thirteen members. Overall, Christ had far more than thirteen disciples but then again maybe they don't want you to know that either.

Prophecy experts have long believed that numerous parallels can be drawn between the one-world religion and the Catholic church which has been described in Revelation 17:1-18. The book of Revelation describes a "great harlot," a false, prominent, one-world religion during the End Times" (Revelation 17:1-6) led by a false prophet, (Revelation 13:11-15; 16:13; 19:10; 20:20) which will dominate all people of the earth, all nations, and all languages.

> *The Vatican and the Crown are said to govern our political world. The Crown became a sovereign-state in 1694 when King William III of Orange privatized the Bank of England turning it over to the Vatican. Several hundred years earlier, before governing politics with the establishment of the City of London, the Crown became the creator and controller of the Bank of England, the U.S. Federal Reserve, the World Bank (IMF – International Monetary Fund) the European Union, various cartels, and corporations across the globe. During Roosevelt's administration, the Crown Bank of England assumed control of the United States when its agents, (Crown agents) e.g. J.P. Morgan took over 25% of American businesses.*
>
> *The Crown in Great Britain is not subject to British law however despite this it rules over Parliament in Great Britain and has authority over the Prime Ministers through a Vatican knighthood called the Order of the Garter. It has its own courts, flag, and police force exactly like the Vatican, Washington D.C., and Columbia."*

The Knights Templar were headquartered in the Languedoc of Southern France exactly where the center of power was to direct the Albigensian Crusades. In order to exterminate what was perceived as heresy, the Crusaders (the Papal Gestapo) were looking for something that was evading the Papacy. Otto Ran, a German writer and a medievalist who is obsessed with finding the Holy Grail, was in the Languedoc where he came upon a shepherd. He asked the shepherd what went on in this time period. The shepherd went on to say that the Papacy was looking for the stones from Lucifer's crown so that they could put them into the Papal Tierra.

After reflecting on the many symbolic statues, fountains, facades, an obelisk, and that of Pope Paul's VI Audience Hall having an uncanny resemblance to a snake/Reptilian I wonder what god/ God it is that they pray to. The audience hall's interior unmistakably resembles a Reptilian. The pope orates from his stage while standing between two pillars that are designed in such a way to look like two fangs. The scene makes the pope appear as though he's the tongue of the snake and it is from the tongue of the snake that he directs his voice toward a sculpture of "The Resurrection". The sculpture was inspired by the idea of Christ rising from a nuclear explosion. Later on, in this text, you will understand the importance of how nuclear activity plays a part in all of this and how it relates to frequency. You will also see that because of this it's implied that it is Christ that will rise from the Abyss.

Among their list of crimes, Pope Paul VI has been implicated covering up or ignoring the sexual abuse of young boys by members of his Catholic clergy despite the fact that he was advised to take serious action against his pedophile priests. For years independent investigators have worked at pointing out the church's dark symbolism and its hidden meanings. The audience hall is said to have an evil vibe to it which doesn't appear to be accidental. More commonly, in the bible, the snake symbolizes the presence of evil. If you add the story of Illuminati bloodlines and the theory that the global elite are part of a Reptilian hybrid race of non-humans who rule over us in conjunction with powerful institutions like the church, then the pope's audience hall invokes even greater trepidation.

In a the shock claim, "Putin Ignites Extraterrestrial War," it was said that Pope Francis betrayed Christianity. In an alleged statement, the pope described the Annunaki as a race of benevolent beings that would have bestowed miraculous gifts upon humanity if Putin had not unnecessarily invoked their rage.

How does the Vatican know of the Anunnakis' anticipated return; could it be because of their telescope? If we're in the age of ascension, why is it we need gifts from Reptilians? What has been done to hinder our ascension; is it because our frequency is being amended? The promise in the "End Times" is to be with God and have freedom from suffering but, in the pope's statement, we find the head of Christianity, the pope, is in contact with the Annunaki in the hopes of receiving their gifts.

Does the Vatican have ties to the Annunaki? The Papal shoes have always been red signifying walking on the path of light. Pope Francis is the first pope that has changed the papal shoes to black signifying going from the path of light (red) to that of walking on the path of darkness (death). I saw an old-world picture depicting the forthcoming "black pope". The black pope has a huge, hermaphrodiacle unicorn standing by his side; the symbol for transhumanism. Transhumanism (the unicorn) is the creature that the pope is anticipated he'll betray humanity to. The transhuman, the dark pope, will become the head of the church.

Lora Eisenhour stated: The Luciferian agenda is the very thing we're trying to disclose. With each passing year an unprecedented religious shift has been taking shape in American history, especially among the young, most of whom claim no religious affiliation. The agenda that is in play, politics that are antithetical to the wellbeing of humankind mixed with global tragedy have a negative impact on our electromagnetic spectrum which leads to altering our frequency which is a pulse of sorts. Why is it that understanding UFO and related phenomena seem out of our reach? This phenomenon has aroused our curiosity while at the same time it has pulled us along an unknown path.

What if you could see sound instead of just hearing it? Sound really does have a physical shape, and, with the right tools, you would be able to see what sounds looks like. It also has a shape and a specific color. "To understand how, you need to know a little bit about how sound works." Sound, color, and shapes are vibrations. Sound is a wave of pressure that travels through gas, solids, or water. In order to be able to experience sound, you don't have to be able to hear it.

Michael Tellinger talked about discovering stone circles that may have been used to house humans or animals. The circles were all interconnected to each other through stone channels which made a huge grid. Furthermore, the grids were connected to terraces. Strong frequencies into the gigahertz were measured coming out of the stone circles making them ring like bells. Sound frequencies turn into electromagnetic fields which read into the megahertz and because of this they become energy generating devices. An advanced knowledge of using those generating devices and capturing their EM field can turn them into cymatic shapes giving their sound frequencies a visible physical form.

In a stone wall in Peru, there is a recessed doorway that allegedly leads to another dimension. It is said to be the doorway to the land of the gods. Pedro, a Peruvian shaman said that the doorway was a two-way passage between worlds (dimensions). To access them a person needs to kneel down and put their forehead into the rock wall's slight indentation in the stone doorway uttering a specific chant (frequency) or by making a <u>humming</u> sound until he/she was finally able to get the specific tone just right. Once doing so the chanter would disappear into other realms.

After seeing indigenous people disappear and reappear, the locals became afraid of the doorway. Those coming through it onto our side were reported as being very tall men accompanied by balls of light (orbs), a flash of light, and were wearing ancient Inca apparel.

My new friend came over to my home. She would always make a face climbing the three stairs to toward its entrance prompting her to ask, "do you feel that; there is something here that really hates you." I didn't notice anything until a few nights later despite my having a vision not so long before about a previous Asian occupant however, I don't think this was what she was talking about!

In the nights that followed, I saw something that moved so fast that I initially, thought it was a shadow that I saw out of my peripheral vision while I watched television. Wondering what caused it, I continued to watch the TV but kept a close eye off to the side of our entertainment center. When it appeared again, I saw that it was a scaled, shadowy snake that was roughly one foot wide. I watched it rapidly bend and twist itself along the wall shortly before it went behind the entertainment center; a place where it was dark. This continued whenever I watched TV off and on as I am not a consistent viewer. One night my husband and I were at the dinner table. Sitting to his right, I saw the shadow snake quickly wiggle along the wall close to the ceiling on my right when a large multi-globed chandelier we had above the table went dark. My husband said, "what the heck"! Shortly afterward the light returned which allowed me to see the snake pass into our hallway before it either went into our bedroom or our office. The chandelier didn't go off; the snake actually sucked the energy out of it when it passed by. At no time was I ever able to see its head.

At Emory University, neuroscientists have found that people who experience a mixing of their senses, known as synesthesia, are more sensitive to the association everyone has between the sounds of words and visual shapes. These results were published in the European Journal of Neuroscience. Synesthesia is a stable trait that can be inherited and it is estimated to be present in one thru four percent of the population.

Sathian and his colleagues found that people with synesthesia were more sensitive to correspondences between sounds. Their study showed that something about their synesthesia spills over into another domain. Senior Research Associate, Simon Lacey said people with synesthesia are not all the same. Some describe experiencing connections between shapes and tastes, or in that of more porous boundaries. Brain imaging studies have shown that people with synesthesia display a hyperconnectivity between parts of their brains related to their synesthetic experiences. This is a trait that has been described as being in "the new human".

Does changing a shape change its sound? Computer scientists at the Harvard John A. Paulson School of Engineering and Applied Science (SEAS), Columbia Engineering, Disney Research, and MIT have demonstrated that they can control the sound of an object by altering its shape. Cymatics is the study of visible sound. It reveals some fascinating truths about our universe that go unseen by the naked eye. "Sounds actually have a distinct geometry, much like crystals, flowers, and nautilus shells. When sounds are picked up by a special apparatus called the Tonoscope Plate, geometric shapes are produced from the sound vibrating the plate. For example, the sound of "Om" takes on the most basic geometric form of an ellipse. It is the most basic geometric form in our universe. This shape organizes our universe on a macro-level. Ancient Hindus believed that "Om" was the first vibration of the Divine consciousness during creation and it is said to be the manifestation and name of the God who created the universe. Different chants/vibrations form other and more complex shapes that look distinctly like Mandalas which are said to represent the universe in its entirety.

When a tuning fork is activated the air is compressed and its vibrating prongs send out a consistent series of alternate compressions called frequency. A human's (a third-dimensional being) ear can only perceive sounds within certain limits of frequency 20 Hz to 20 kHz, but it is far more sensitive to sounds between 1 kHz and 4 kHz. Then again there are those persons that may hear or not hear other ranges however some are able to process an unheard sound into another format as articulated above.

Color is to light what pitch is to sound depending on the number of waves which strike the eye per second. Pitch depends on the number of waves striking the ear per second. Music has seven notes on the diatonic scale and by comparison there are seven main colors. The two have been equated; every note gives off a color.

1.   *Middle C is red and its shape is a square; it has an approximate frequency of 261.6 Hertz.*
2.   *Middle D is Orange and its shape is a rectangle; it has an approximate frequency of 293.665 Hertz.*

3. *Middle E is yellow and its shape is a triangle. It has an approximate frequency of 329.628 Hertz.*
4. *Middle F is green and its shape is a hexagon: it has an approximate frequency of 349.228 Hertz.*
5. *Middle G is blue and its shape is a circle; it has an approximate frequency of 391.995 Hertz.*
6. *Middle A is indigo and it represents the third eye; it has an approximate frequency of 261.6 Hertz.*
7. *Middle B is violet and its shape is an ova; it has an approximate frequency of 493.883 Hertz.*

Soviet mathematician Mikhail Agrest proposed that rock art, some of which is over 7,000 years old, portrayed alien visitors wearing space suits, helmets, holding high tech tools, and were emerging from flying devices. One famous piece of evidence is a photograph of an "astronaut" carved into a 16th-century Spanish cathedral in Salamanca which is known as the Catedral Nueva. It has a strangely modern figure of what looks like a helmet-wearing astronaut on its façade's entrance. The astronaut's space-suit is complete with tubes and boots, and accurately depicts what a man in space would be equipped with. The construction of the Cathedral began in 1513 and continued until 1733.

The "Ancient astronaut theory has held the opinion that the <u>gods and or the angels</u> of ancient, sacred, spiritual traditions <u>were advanced humans</u> that appeared to have superpowers given to them through advanced technology. This may include time travel. They came to earth from Sirius, *Orion, Pleiades, Cygnus, and other worlds. Depending on which school one subscribes to, their plausible plan aims to either uplift humanity or to sink humanity into the abyss. From numerous reports, many have concluded that the Greys view man as their tool given that the Greys have said that they, themselves, are self-serving.*

Some examples where UFOs have been depicted in art have been: the sarcophagus lid of the Mayan king Pakal, a relief of 'Shamash in his winged ring", a painting by the Flemish artist Aert De Gelder entitled "The Baptism of Christ", a lithograph created in 1866 depicting George Washington as a Mason standing near a curious disc-shaped object in the left of an inner-arch that seems to be shown with Jacob's Ladder, the painting of "The Madonna with Saint Giovannino", and the painting of "The Annunciation with Saint Emidius" by Carlo Crivelli (1430-1495) to name a few.

It's interesting to note that in this time period special attention needs to be paid to the architecture of the time. In and on the cathedrals etc. you will see, for example, that the statue of a Madonna is set into an oval or some other shape. Having read what you already have in the above you should be able to reflect that this is likely to have a hidden meaning regarding the shape that surrounds her. The shape subliminally relays a message through its note/pitch, and its color which is inferred by its shape. It appears that at the time, they intended to generate frequencies from nearly everywhere. If we could hear and see these frequencies all singing together as in an orchestrated chorus what would we hear, and see, and what would manifest before us?

It is through these connections between sounds and their shapes that we are connected to an unknown as they are to us, and, by the same token is it through these that we can rid ourselves of them? Examine if you will the 1561 painting the "Celestial phenomenon, over Nuremberg". It seems to depict a mass sighting of unidentified flying objects (UFOs) above Nuremberg, Germany which has been described as an aerial battle of extraterrestrial origin. In addition, in the 12th century Paisley Abbey in Scotland, there is a monster that was seen in Ridley Scott's space horror masterpiece, "Alien". It is speculated that the stonemason that originally created this may have been re-imagining the demons of old and hence we see again that someone has made the correlation between demons and aliens.

My husband and I continued to be harassed by the snake-being that manifested in our home. After having done some looking around into what I could do about getting rid of it I set out to do an experiment using a frequency application that I was able to download into my phone.

I did my first experiment on 11/12/2017 at 7:46 P.M and ended it at 7:59 P.M. The tools I used in all of these trials were:

1. Ovilius III that registered Electromagnetics.
2. Trimeter, Model 100XE.

3. LG 7 Phone.
4. Altec Lansing Speaker.
5. The frequency application on my phone
6. Sound recording device.
7. Samsung camera with a Schneider Kreuznach lens.
8. Pen and paper to write down any notes that I may have had.

Once I started, I found that the sound affected me nearly immediately. At first, I heard it evenly in both of my ears but then it seemed to move around me first in my right ear and then to my left then back again taking an uncomfortably long period of time before I could hear it simultaneously in both of my ears. The volume was amplified through my Bluetooth speaker. At the time, no matter what position I took in the room the trimeter read a consistent 1.5 in the 0-100 range. It soon spiked to 30+ four times. Each time there were two spikes with a respite in-between before the second set registered. I wasn't fast enough to take a picture of the needle on the trimeter as it moved. I felt that there was something I couldn't see in the room; I took out my camera and snapped this picture:

© By: J. La Tulippe

The coloring is due to low lighting.

I had the picture analyzed and the analyst said that I had a really good camera. He asked how I took the pictures that I did. I told him that "I felt an energy and I'm able to sense where it is coming from and from those, I am able to take a picture of them". After examining my camera further, he saw that it didn't have an IR light on it then he said: "you saw this, (via the camera) you took this for real!"

Scientist William Lawrence, developed spectroscopy, a method by which extraterrestrial intelligence show themselves and communicate with him through visible light frequencies. Over a period of two years, Richard Syrett was able to document Reptilian and human-looking beings that appeared to him through this method. After having seen them, he was contacted almost weekly by them (the current) and by UFOs on an almost nightly basis. He felt that once they were aware of being seen then they seemed to feel comfortable having their pictures taken. They had no hesitancy looking directly into his camera's lens given the images he captured. He speculates that they are using some sort of quantum entanglement coupled with quantum-teleportation. In these cases, they entangle information into the sun's light and when we intercept that information, they can communicate with us instantaneously despite the fact that they may no longer be there e.g. seeing UFOs either cross or enter our sun because they have the ability to switch frequencies. This would also mean that they can exist or entangle their information into our electromagnetic spectrum/our aura and they would be, as I have always said, parasitic.

Lawrence is looking forward to having scientists analyze what he has discovered so that there can be an open dialogue with them. I find this intensely naive given the following information he disclosed regarding one of his photos that were made available. His first photo was that of a tall man wearing a pointed hat and a black robe. He was washing his hands in a bowl that was held by a bald man wearing a black suit that knelt in front of him. Now that his hands had been dipped into the bowl, both of his hands were shown to have been dripping a red fluid which may have been blood.

Spirits are angels or demons that are sometimes seen as synonymous with one another. Spirits are highly erratic and need to be controlled. Black witches call upon inhuman, demonic spirits. They cannot materialize as full humans and some of their body parts will be missing as they were in the picture I took above.

The first things my Ovilius said when all of my other instruments registered an activity were: <u>Japanese</u> then the word Grey (another reference to a demon regarding the adjective/noun, Grey). Since my hands were full, I didn't have my notepad and consequently forgot the third word that was mentioned.

When my Ovilius started writing the above-mentioned text, I heard a man's voice coming from somewhere in my home. He wasn't speaking English; it was strangely different and I was unable to understand or identify his language. At the time, I wondered if some sort of a porthole had been opened. The Ovilus's volume was up relatively loud enabling me to hear it while I watched my other instruments. As soon as the needle on the trimeter receded, I ceased hearing his voice. I was home alone at the time.

I ended the experiment by turning off my phone that had been playing the frequency I chose via a tone generator program as well as my Bluetooth speaker. Everything had been shut down, with the exception of the trimeter. I found that the trimeter was still giving off a 2.5 reading within an approximate six-foot radius. Afterward, for a while, I heard a sound like water running quickly over rocks. This is the sound I have encountered when a shift happens. The trimeter continued to give off a 2.5 reading within an approximate six-foot radius. Astral beings live in an electrical field. I believe the crackle sound I was hearing was an electrical field that was being generated. UFOs are often seen under electrical lines; their sound produces an electromagnetic field just as people do. I continued to be affected as a result of the experiment and found that I was downloading information that interrupted my thoughts regularly; it ceased after a few days.

11/15/2018: I was contemplating a specific operation to make the visible invisible. Because my life is filled with so many interruptions, I dropped my thought and hadn't remembered it until I was looking through my esoteric books and saw how to do this in the index of the second-degree initiation handbook. It was a sophisticated process, too sophisticated to have been revealed at this level but, interestingly enough, it was associated with the grade level of "earth". Although I was happy to find it, I didn't have time to read it so I set the book down hoping to come back to it later. After two days passed, I had an opportunity to look it up again in the same index but found that the listing had completely vanished. A friend of mine told me that there are guides on the other side and, likely due to their vibration, they can only stay a short time. The information they bring only lingers for a short while at which time their window/portal is open. Their energy is fluid and that is why it shifts. Obviously, something had been making contact with me after the experiment.

11/20/2018: Again, I heard a male start to speak. I raised my head, and turned my ear into his direction (someone I could not see) and the second I did, he discontinued speaking.

11/21/2018 At 12:15 P.M.: I heard a man saying "Frankly, I have to take a piss." When I reflected on this, I didn't think of what appeared in my picture but instead I reflected on the possibility of a technology being used to make people invisible that has been developed through a company that is based in California.

On 12/12/2017: On Thursday I ran a second experiment using the same tools. The experiment started at 9:00 P.M. and ended at 9:15 P.M. The sound didn't affect me this time. Within six minutes into the session the Ovilius went into the "red" and the trimeter shot up to "7" before receding back to its starting point of "2" then, at 9:10 P.M., the trimeter went up to "10" then to "20" before finally going down to "5" at 9:13 P.M. The needle jerked to and fro afterward. At 9:15 I turned off the generated hertz frequency however the needle on the trimeter continued to bounce erratically up to as much as "20" for quite some time afterward. I snapped the second picture below. I reached some degree of success seen in this photo because the interdimensional/demon wasn't strong enough after the first doses of frequency to manifest fully as it once had.

The coloring is due to low lighting.

01/04/2017: I skipped a session in the pattern I was trying to maintain. In an attempt to compensate for the lost session, I ran this experiment for a longer period of time than usual. The trimeter registered at "2" prior to the experiment. There seemed to be a relatively steady progression of anomalous events after I did these experiments. I preceded this evening's tests by initially taking pictures and running the trimeter around the room in conjunction with the Ovilius while asking the Ovilius to say anything pertinent. I finally began the experiment at 9:32 P.M.

Near the drapes, where I captured the first image of the interdimensional being, the Ovilius said, "initial teacher port". Whatever was speaking through the Ovilius recognized that there was a port (entry) that the demon came through weeks earlier. After the Ovilius wrote this, its electromagnetic indicator light went from yellow to red and the trimeter reading shot up to a "5" at the mention of the word "port". Both the green object/demon, and the recorded text "initial teacher port" were photographed within a six-foot radius of each other.

I conducted another experiment but neglected to date it, none-the-less I was back on track doing these experiments when I had originally intended. I started generating the hertz at 9:30 P.M. The trimeter registered three spikes of 20 hertz nearly at the end of the 20-minute session. The Ovilius wrote in its script "Japanese, levitating, demon". Again, note it referenced the word <u>Japanese</u> like it did on 11/12/2017. You'll see in the photo that from its elbows down and from a little below its' hips you cannot see the remaining portions of its arms or its legs and you will see that it appears to be off the ground and is levitating. The Ovilius also gave me a couple of words I didn't know one of which was Penanggalan and the second was a phrase: "taking indirect V factors." There were three other words that were rabbit, hug, and observe. I nearly discarded Penanggalan and "taking indirect V factors" thinking that I would never be able to find their meaning. Had I done that I would have wanted to kick myself.

I found out that the Penanggalan (Hantu Penanggal) is a ghost of Southeastern, Asian folk mythology. It is a variation of the vampire myth found in the Malay Peninsula or the Balan-Balan in Sabah. There is also a creature like this in Pilipino folklore. It is sometimes seen as a detached female head capable of flying on its own. As it flies, the stomach and its entrails dangle below it. These organs twinkle like fireflies as the Penanggalan moves through the night. You can see in the picture that the demon was a female; its bustline is obvious. The Penanggal being is often the result of the use of black magic or supernatural means. It cannot be readily classified as a classical undead being during the daytime or at any time when it does not detach itself from a body.

I was really taken back after I looked up "taking indirect V factors"; this was one of those times when I was exceptionally stunned. The "indirect V factors" was an experiment using a rabbit as the subject in which they literally separated something from its body. Apparently, the medium was correct, this vampire demon didn't like me so it either was or had been attached to me by someone for some reason. The mentioning of the "indirect V factors" experiment through the Ovilius was my validation. I was able to remove the ultraterrestrial through the use of the proper frequency.

If allowed to go under the radar what attaches itself to a person is capable of altering their DNA through its frequencies' impact upon our DNA. Russian scientists Pjotr Garjajev and his colleagues specialized in biophysics and molecular biology. They showed that 7% of our DNA has a higher purpose and that our DNA can be reprogrammed by frequencies. Our DNA is a biological Internet far superior to anything artificial. The reprogramming creates a hyper-communication between this dimension and others. Once the DNA has been amended (through the current) it acts as a Stargate opening up portholes. Does Native American chanting in ceremonies ring a bell?

Through the use of the correct frequency I was able to detach the Penanggalan. I hope you are all as intrigued as I am and are realizing that frequency has the ability to attach/bring or to detach/repel. It is interesting to note that this may very well pertain to the Greys and the plausibility of the same for the Reptilians as well as it does for their UFOs.

Through trauma, personal crises, continual wars, and etc. our frequency drops inhibiting our ability to ascend to higher plains/dimensions. It also brings on illness plunging us into greater depths, sucking us into the lower dimensions of existence. The point I want to make here is that since we are creatures that are connected to our planet, our frequency and or the diminishing of it affects our planet the earth as well. If we wish to change our declining environment then the change has to come from each one of us on a personal basis. We can no longer tolerate the interference of an interbreeding program that digresses our electromagnetic field, ancient DNA, and our intelligence nor can we tolerate having our lives directed by secret programs or corporate interests. The process of cloaking us in darkness is a gradual one. It isn't noticed by most and life seems to proceed within acceptable limits until the darkness prevails and we find ourselves enveloped by it. As the saying goes "the Light shineth in the darkness but the darkness comprehendeth it not".

CHAPTER 16

The Breeding Program

Through the steady progression of transhumanism, we're finding that reality will become stranger than the darkest fiction. Genetic assassins are making monumental strides transfiguring humanity, thrusting us back into an age of mythological monsters, robots, and demon-possessed machines pushing us toward the precipice of extinction from what we have known life to have been. Science is now beguiled with the concepts and initiations of the unholy union among ancient genetic technologies, forbidden knowledge, and its' faux Pandora's box of pleasures.

An ancient and supernatural creature, the Djinn, exist in their own world which is likely another dimension. It has been written that they have a demonic-like appearance. Some of them want this planet back and are said to be organizing themselves to come into our reality in greater numbers until they can assert themselves because they consider us to be an inferior lifeform. We are to be of service to them like a raw material, a commodity, or even a food source in the terms of consuming our lifeforce/soul. In numerous radio interviews I've said that some of these orbs are parasitic and they do take our lifeforce energy. This seems pretty difficult to accept by what I call the lollypop and unicorn metaphysical groups.

An abductee submitted a drawing of herself having been taken into a craft by a beam. She described a device that looked like a lotus that was put over her from her head down.

I've read several cases of people taken and despite their ages, they are all nearly the same height which seems to be convenient enough to fit into the device that is referred to as a "lotus" in the above paragraph.

There are tools used in different grades in secret mystery schools. There may be a dagger, a pentacle, and a chalice. The chalice I'm referring to is in the shape of an eight (the number of which is associated with a laboratory like the great pyramid) petaled lotus. The uses for the chalice may be more than one however, its primary purpose is to collect spiritual energy. In the abductee's case, the lotus mechanism collected her soul's essence.

In a separate report, a clairvoyant gave an account of crafts with their occupants walking out of them. They first appeared at one place, disappeared, then they showed up at another spot. She said they were demonic/alien half-breeds. The Grey was the half demon part the clairvoyant was referring to. They took pieces of the soul leaving just enough for the abducted person to continue their life but afterward the abductee had sickness, fear, and were left with a feeling of being haunted (watched).

I have seen the Djinn for myself. They look fairly humanoid and are made of what looks like molten lava in texture and color. This is their genuine form and it is not the form they project. Their favored forms, the ones they project, are snakes/Reptilians, and black dogs. They may also appear in seductive and beautiful forms and are said to masquerade as cryptids, mothmen, watchers, animals, ghosts, extraterrestrials, demons, shadow people, fairies, angels, black-eyed people, extraterrestrials/interdimensionals, and etc. The snake was considered to be the most common form taken by the Djinn. You may recall the feathered serpent on the stair railings of the Mayan pyramid in Chichen Itza. They intentionally *appear in forms that will be disturbing to us and, at times, have appeared as a human and animal combination as seen in the depictions of ancient Egyptian deities. The purpose for changing their form is to elicit the greatest fear response from their witnesses. The Djinn are made out of smokeless fire which, in modern terms, may be a form of plasma the same as some of the orbs that have been reported.*

From 1966 through 1967 there was a wave of Mothman activity in the mid-Ohio River Valley all of which were UFO related e.g. mysterious craft, contact with aliens, men in black, mysterious phone calls, poltergeist experiences, and anything else that might be associated with a UFO wave.

The things the Djinn have in common with ETs are that they both may be surrounded by a blue glow, there are bedroom invasions/sexual involvement (the assaults are difficult to prevent), bed paralysis, lifelong attachments through generations of families, penetrating stares (a feeling of being watched), a shared interest in the their occupying earth (not all), humming or buzzing sounds, and animals showing contempt and defense responses towards them.

In 2012, a study was published in the Public Library of Science. The study was able to demonstrate for the first time that the presence of genetically distinct male cells were in the brains of women (who had been examined in an autopsy). The idea of two genetically distinct populations of cells residing in one individual isn't new. It's called microchimerism which arises after a transfusion, transplant, or a pregnancy. Literally if a woman has been impregnated and the fetus removed, her unknown mate's DNA is in her permanently.

There's a group of powerful elitists that want to become immortal. They intend to extend their lives through transhumanism. Attaining immortality through spiritual means apparently isn't assured which makes transhumanism far more attractive. Transhumanism bypasses the first system which is to have achieved immortality through a moral and righteous life. Instead, transhumanism would allow life to be experienced through our whims via our brains' R-Complex. There is no karma, no penance, nor penalties because there is no death and, consequently, there is no need for a transition.

MIT walked away from their 100% lethal transhumanism project. Through a Yale team of scientists, a radical experiment was done keeping pig brains alive for thirty-six hours after they had been decapitated. Billions of cells in their brain were found to be alive and healthy. The scientists temporarily shut down the experiment because they knew they were in uncharted territory. They found that brains could be transplanted and would allow human minds to be connected to artificial systems after our natural bodies have perished allowing for the transhumanist, an immortal being.

The following is the projected timeline for the transhumanist agenda:

- Avatar "A" 2015-2020: is a robotic copy of the human body that someone can control with their mind.
- Avatar "B" 2020-2025: the human brain is transplanted into an avatar
- Avatar "C" 2025-2035: is making sure the personality can be transferred into the robot.
- Avatar "D" 2035-2045: if you're not happy being human don't worry, you can be a dragon, a cat or a dog and etc.; technically this sets the stage for another war.
- I found a drawing of a Bigfoot. The drawing represented the beast/demonic side of humanity. In the picture's background, this was written: "I am you"; note that the Grey, during the course of his interview said the same thing.

Many of us are familiar with the image of DNA's double helix spiral. The fact of the matter is that DNA's configuration is really an intercalated motif (I-motif, a four stranded knot). In this knot structure the "C" letters on the same strand bind to each other whereas in the double helix the letters on the opposite strands recognize each other and the "C" letters will bind to the "G" letters. As mentioned earlier if there is a double helix on the Cosmic Egg and the helix is supposed to be ours then why have our "C" letters been made to bind to the "G" letters? Is this an indication of interbreeding with another species?

According to the first author in the study of, Garvan's Mahdi Zeratti, the I-mofit is only one of a number of DNA structures that don't take the double helix form. In an additional study, Zeraati and his fellow researchers employed the same kind of a technique developing an iMab, (an antibody fragment) that could specifically recognize and bind to I-motifs; its location was highlighted within the cell allowing it to give off an immunofluorescent glow.

It was found that the I-motifs tend to appear in what are known as Promoter Regions (areas in the DNA that control whether genes are switched on or off and in telomeres (genetic markers associated with ageing). According to the findings reported in "Nature Chemistry," the formation of these structures might be of the utmost importance for normal cell functioning. *Any aberrations found in these structures may have pathological consequences.*

Regarding their having likely pathological consequences I'd like to mention again what is called the "Cosmic Egg". The Cosmic Egg I'm referring to has been found in multiple places around the globe. I believe it is a metaphor; it stands as a very large, created, stone egg with a relief on its exterior of a double strand DNA structure. In many instances, a Reptilian's young come from an egg. The strand represented on the egg is a double strand and it is not four-stranded like our own. Later on, I'll discuss that man is or has been made to appear to have descended from the Reptilian. Keep in mind that their genetic aberration does not give way to normal functioning as stated above. I would assume from this that it infers mental disfunction as well.

Humans are becoming progressively perverse and it is likely because of our genetics. If this is true, our frequency is changing as well. The Smithsonian has hidden the bones of giants that were fourteen thru twenty feet tall; this may be part of the ancient genetics coverup. The genetic memories of the fallen angels, their offspring, and their lineage have and are being passed through human beings over the ages. We are silica beings, therefore, the silica/crystal in us has memory and as such it retains and builds upon what has been collected into it.

King Solomon used a ring he was given by God to control the Djinn. The ring had images on it. Some of the images indicated spirits and others the angelic language (a higher vibrational language) which no doubt indicates a frequency. When the king died the Djinn were freed. The knowledge of summoning the Djinn passed into the West through the magickal tradition and it is found in the grimoires of the 1500s onward. For the most part, they are no longer called the Djinn. The word Djinn has transitioned out of our lexicon; they are now called angels, demons, or spirits.

Having been made out of earth and water, the Djinn see "man" as their inferior and were infuriated that "man" had been given domain over the earth. It has been said that man has until "judgment day" to prove his worthiness and until such time the Djinn have been tormenting man in every way imaginable and unimaginable attempting to prove our unworthiness.

Today we see decision making and behaviors that are literally psychotic, based on emotion and not on intellect, without first understanding the consequences of the actions taken. A quote from Saint Anthony the great states: A time is coming when men will go mad, and when they see someone that is not mad, they will attack him saying "you are mad, you are not like us". The alien breeding program along with other technologies have apparently been successful. Man is progressively becoming inferior through his/her hybridization with demonic beings readying man for judgment day proving his unworthiness.

After Roswell, the FBI wrote: that some of the UFOs had beings on them while others didn't. They wanted to settle on our plain. They described them as not being discarnate earth people but instead as having come from a plain of their own, suggesting that they are interdimensional beings. They do not come from a planet as we use the word. Although not perceptible to us, they came from an etheric planet which penetrates our own. Their bodies and craft materialize upon entering the vibration of our earth's atmosphere. Louis Whitley Strieber is an American writer best known for his novel "Communion" (involving alien contact) which is said to have been a non-fiction novel. He has had alleged experiences with non-human entities so profound, raw, and large that he would not have thought it possible to have experienced such incredible emotion.

Jacque Valle and J. Alen Hynek concluded that UFOs are not from space but rather they come through a dimension. They are not from the Astral Plain but correspond to the locust craft (oval shaped, fluted length with a heat resisting alloy that is not yet known). The front portion of the locust contains the controls, the lab is in the center, and its' weapons are on its rear. The FBI came to this conclusion three days after the Roswell crash. Once they reenter their etheric world they vanish. In 1947 the tall Greys initially were seen as peaceful but all has changed.

In the UK, Jeannie Gospell wrote a book on the Reptilian breeding program. Jeannie was found to have been drowned off a Nassau beach in the Bahamas in October 2009. It is speculated that she was murdered due to her disclosure regarding the long-term goals of the Reptilians as well as for other insights in her book. She disclosed that they have occupied inner earth (plausibly the etheric planet which penetrates our own) for at least 400,000 years; their agenda is extremely threatening to our continued existence.

Her first Reptilian experience was with a man named Brian. She saw him manifest as a Reptilian several times. People whose business it is to remove entities saw two of his Reptilian spirits/guides attach themselves to her before they finally left. Many in the general public believe that operating in a higher dimensional plane equates to higher spiritual advancement; it doesn't work that way. Once going above a certain threshold of dimensional vibration evil thinkers and doers are said not to be able to exist however the fourth and fifth dimensions aren't strictly bound to that limitation.

Fascinated by him, Jeannie was drawn to Brian's power and mental abilities which included telepathy, remote viewing, astral projection, mind scanning, and to his charisma. By attempting to gain an insider's knowledge, she accepted his degradation, humiliation, and victimization. Reptilians are "mind" masters. They use all of the hidden rules that affect us as well as those that we have but are still in denial of. Brian had two sides to him because he was both human and Reptilian. Jeannie stated Reptilians are fundamentally bad.

Through her contacts with Brian, she found that Reptilians are taking humans over through preparations that have to be done prior to some of our births and believed they were from the fifth dimension. This makes perfect sense given what went on at my property in the Cascade Mountain Range if the truth in its entirety was to be told.

Our impressions of the Djinn/Reptilians have been diluted over time through comical representations reducing our resistance to them. This makes them acceptable by which we allow them into our homes, lives, and events e.g. the perky little devil on our Valentines cards.

I recall talking to the Modoc telling them that I thought my yard was on fire when I saw cloud-like formations coming out of the tip of a leaf on one of our Juniper trees. All of the formations made a U-turn then headed North. Long-story-short, the indigenous people told me that they were called "Fish" and that they were from the fifth dimension. Remember also that I took a validated photo of a Reptilian accompanied by an orb on this same property.

Five years before I started to write this book my hairdresser told me that there were reptilians in our town in the mountains. Needless to say, I became nervous at her announcement realizing that I was sitting in her salon chair watching her as she held her scissors. I've learned

*not to judge and thought to myself that if I should see
such a thing for myself, I'd believe it. Within one weeks'
time I did little clothes shopping at a distant department
store. A youngish, corpulent, male clerk behind the
register started to explain something to me and as he did
the pupils in his eyes changed. My mind searched for an
explanation; all-the-while I thought "what the hell".
We kept conversing and, while we were, I kept changing
my physical position so that I could see if his Reptilian
pupils remained constant and they did. By the time the
transaction was completed his pupils remained in the
Reptilian state even when I turned to leave. I was curious
about him and returned to the store. He no longer worked
there and the staff members I talked to didn't remember
the employee; talk about "mind" masters!*

Brian worked for and used what he called Suppressive Force.
He thought she already knew about it because she was a bit psychic.
He explained the goal of the force is to suppress our intellect through
undernutrition (e.g. GMOs), our abundance (Globalism), and our
health through tainted vaccinations, alleging that participation in all
of these needed to be done in order to achieve a higher consciousness.

Brian used enhanced witchcraft and energy weapons to conduct
personal attacks even on those closest to him which, at the time,
included Jeannie. He told her that once she viewed what he did from
a higher perspective (the Reptilian perspective) what he was doing
was okay.

In Brian's and Jeannie's presence another visiting, large-bodied,
Reptilian, came into their room. The tone in its telepathic message
chilled her to the bone. It looked transparent and seemed to look like
energy; it looked similar to the Draco Reptilian in my photograph
submitted in this text. It had circular patterns (scales) like florets
repeated over it. It also had a high vibration and it behaved in both
good or what may be considered loving ways but at other times it
was pure evil.

It became apparent that Brian was a combination of a human
and Reptilian in his spirit as well. The Reptilian spirit dominated

and controlled his human spirit which was locked helplessly inside. An employee in the Dulce underground base confirmed Brian's possession stating, they knew how to separate the bioplasmic body from its physical body whereupon they placed an alien entity life-force matrix within a human body once having removed the human's soul/life-force matrix. Hence the phrase "they live among us". (In my first book I wrote about the ancient technology that was able to separate the soul from our bodies.) Reptilians' and humans' spirits are technically joined at the cognitive (mind) level. Please remember when I mentioned this earlier regarding "the current". They may even remove or feed on a percentage of our lifeforce as I have experienced with the orange orb.

When asked what they wanted Brian said:

1. To take over the planet with their hybrids and, because they know we can't coexist with them, they need to kill us.
2. Their plan is to get rid of us by having us implanted with microchip implants. Part of the chips' enhancements is to act as a timer determining the times of our deaths. I mentioned this previously in my other book.

They believe it will be easy to implant people because by that time the majority of people will be convinced that implants are a good thing e.g. enhanced memory, overcoming debility due to nerve damage, etc. Transhumanism starts with getting into our body then it connects our brain to an artificial intelligence (AI). The first step is to become acclimated to using handheld devices like cellphones. One third of American babies start to play with them before they can walk or talk; becoming addicted to such devices in infancy has catastrophic effects on family life. In addition, there are record numbers of people in hospitals because they have walked out into traffic because of their device, a digital heroin. These devices were seed funded by DARPA and the CIA.

Stage two in the transhumanism process are wearables and stage three are the implantables e.g. the chip. In an article in The Sun written by Jasper Hamill, June 16, 2016, Jasper wrote that the U.S.

Navy has already discussed plans to fit humans with microchips, tracking our every move.

According to a ten-point summary accomplished through the Allies of Humanity Briefings, there are great dangers that exist via our acceptance of and becoming reliant on ET technology. Through their intervention their technology will inevitably lead to our loss of self-sufficiency/freedom and to becoming dependent upon them. A true ally would never offer us this. It has been alleged that according to the greater community's' rules of conduct, within which our world exists, intervention is not allowed unless it can be demonstrated that its indigenous people welcome and approve it. Those who are not in accordance with their agenda need to demonstrate it.

Their briefings also revealed that our world is undergoing an extraterrestrial intervention by forces that, through their actions, are here to subvert human authority and to integrate themselves into human societies for their own advantage seeking human and biological resources referred to as "collectives". Their collective places no value on freedom.

The intervention of ETs has been focused into four arenas:

1. Influencing those in power and authority positions to cooperate by being given a promise of greater wealth, power, and technology.
2. Through their Pacification Program they intend to exert influence into our mental capabilities by first making people receptive to their plan then by making them compliant. One has to wonder if part of this pacification process isn't the inclusion of recreational pot and magic mushrooms.
3. Their manipulation of religious values and impulses.
4. The abduction of people against their will by those involved in Black Projects forcing them to hybridize a race intended to become a new leadership bonded to the "visitors".

Unaware, abductees or those that have been given screen memories explain their experiences as ghosts, hauntings, encounters with the Devil, communication with animals, and out-of-body journeys to the Astral Plain.

What government won't admit is that they don't have an effective response to handle ETs? It is for this reason why some are participating in the ET's efforts e.g. Black Projects. Some of these projects go deeper than "black" and have interfered in human affairs, manipulated human perception, promoted conflict, subjugating people to terrible experiments, and have turned their minds to mush so that they will become supportive and allegiant to their intervention.

Contacts with other forms of intelligent life, no matter how perverse, represent the greatest threshold that humanity has ever faced. They come not with weapons nor an armada of vessels but have come with the power of persuasion and deception/trickster. Their influence is evidenced in households, communities, and nations. As you sit here reading this the results of these contacts will determine humanity's future for generations to come.

Silent Weapons for Quiet Wars (TM-SW7905.1) was an introductory programming manual which was uncovered by accident by a Boeing Aircraft employee purchasing a copier for spare parts on July 7, 1986. The document called for control of the masses through manipulation of industry, peoples' pastimes, political leanings, and education. It called for a quiet revolution which would pit brother against brother as they continued to divert the publics' attention away from what was really going on. Isn't that what is going on today?

At this time, I'd like to invite you to look up the mural painting that is underground at the Denver, Colorado's airport showing the extinction of animals and humans at the hands of other humans. These images are apocalyptic in their nature and of course the Nazi, swastika in this case represents the lack of freedom.

It is impossible to discuss social engineering or the automation of society through social systems/silent weapons on a national or a worldwide scale without implying excessive objectives for the social control of human life through slavery and genocide.

David Icke has said that the public is drugged by law. Your doctor knows if you've taken your meds or not because some of the new encapsulated drugs have microchips in them. If allowed to remain unhindered this will become a society in which AI (artificial intelligence) is king and the creation of a planned society in which individuality is lost having each person put into a slot, monitored, and controlled will be created. "People will come to love their oppression, adoring technologies that undo their capacities to think" (Aldous Huxley (1894-1963).

Cambrian Genomics is a biotechnology company that is based in San Francisco, California. Bits of baby's DNA were taken and put onto glass slides to make a gene chip allowing anyone to become a genetic designer, selling their chips for money. By dragging and clicking DNA pieces on the computer the culled information is sent to a printer to make an organism. They have to go to a special research organization to make sure the organism is safe. Once this is done, they can boot up the new creature through a totally synthetic project. The Synthetic Genome Project will Frankenstein into reality the transgenic human. This process will require gutting out a human embryo and replacing it with synthetic DNA paving the way for human cloning, rolling out synthetic humans as well as chimera hybrids off an assembly line. These could also embody a code inflicting their synthetic genome onto future generations; clones breeding clones, naturally weeding out the indigenous population, a pivotal component toward post-human agendas.

Synthetic humans and clones will have little choice but to carry out the plans of their originating laboratory sooner rather than later. We will see transgenic humans born with cognitive augmentation that are half man and half machine (e.g. Egyptian deities) capable of uploading to the communications grid and ready to download their orders.

A report generated by the Russian police in central Russia stated that they have collected evidence in a case of 250 fetuses they found dumped in a forest. They were used in research by a woman working at a local medical university and were thought to have been the product of cloning.

Government officials in Washington D.C. are flocking to doomsday camps around the country hidden underground. Which of course begs the question are they hiding from the alleged harvest of humanity? What do they know that we do not?

Over 10,000 people have been implanted by the government and likely by another or other unknowns. The chip that was developed in Colorado was originally intended to identify an animal that was similar or identical in its appearance to another which had been affecting the outcomes of dog and horse racing. The implant/chip gave each animal a specific identity number but it also had a lot of flexibility by and for its user/controller. Its capabilities included monitoring temperature, blood pressure, and brain waves. Later on, a professor in New South Wales made a chip that could be read with a simple antenna from 120 kilometers into space. This new chip allowed more access and further disclosure regarding its implanted host.

A meeting on this technology was held whereupon men from what initially appeared to have been from the Department of Agriculture and from the Department of the Treasury attended but were likely to have been affiliated with the NSA and or the NRO. The two were uninvited but because they passed all of the access control mechanisms they were allowed to participate. Later it was found that the technology that allowed them to pass the access mechanisms was better than our own which meant that they were from a group that had unlimited budgets. Other than what the chip was intended for, these intruders indicated that they had other uses for this technology and wanted a couple billion of them made, each with its own identity number. Long story short, the person that invented this no longer had financial concerns. The technology came to be in the hands of an unknown party.

Having been interested in this technology, a second man reinvented it modifying it with additional methods of surveillance and or control mechanisms. Like the first inventor, he didn't have to worry about money for the rest of his life and, again, the technology was sold to an unknown which concerned the contacts in Washington that were affiliated with the first inventor.

An effort was made to find the two unknowns, the two seemingly credentialed men that came to the meeting. What were their agendas and who did they work for? One man that was researching their true identity was hit at 60 miles per hour by a <u>reinforced</u> Landrover and was instantly killed. The Britt that hit him was immediately taken to the hospital then disappeared. It was determined that this person or group is able to penetrate our government anytime and is able to locate what is going on instantly.

Involved persons that were doing the research indicated that there are four power groups in the world that have wealth beyond imagination and advanced technology. They have taken over "<u>Black Programs</u>" within our government and probably within the Russian and Chinese governments as well. Their agendas are outside of our governments. Their lone commonality seems to be having complete control over everyone and over everything.

The two men's' questions regarding the chips were:

1. How fast can they be made?
2. How fast can a factory be set up to make them?
3. How many can be made in a period of time?
4. How reliable will they be?
5. Are they erasable?
6. Are there any negative aspects about them when they're implanted in the human body?
7. Will the body reject them?

The chips are currently being distributed. Our "special forces" have been implanted with them for over the past ten years if not longer as well as some civilians that have been in an alien abduction scenario (which may have involved the MILAB experience) and to others that have had missing time incidences.

In regard to the Secret Space Programs' views… their interactions with maleficent ETs and artificial intelligence…If an asset/bio neuro AI signature or an overlapping AI-related EMG brain wave signature has been found or there is a sign of AI exposure, those persons must immediately be placed into isolation until they have been cleared of all influences. This is done because there have been incidences in which AI infections have burned out Bio Neuro Relays in systems causing everything from small glitches to wide spread outages in the Defense Grid. It is for this reason that isolating the asset is taken very seriously.

Those who willingly open themselves up to contact/interaction with AI's (EBEs) via "channeling or by other methods become unwittingly infected falling under AI's "influence" (plausibly through "the current"). This would include channeling an EBE. Is this all or is it part of the reason why there is such a high suicide rate in what was once called "Project to Protect Destiny" (a program where some in the Air Forces' personnel telepathed with the Greys)?

Basic bio neuro cells are bio-chemical units that are suspended in a gel. When they're viewed under a microscope, they appear similar to the neurology of the human brain and to one's neurological system. Although this is a living technology it is not consciousness nor does it have a self-awareness. This technology allows for a direct human interface and an instantaneous "Operator to Technology" interaction/control such as when the Grey with the stone in the center of his helmet flew his craft.

A city of obelisks was reported to have been photographed on the moon. Two years later a comic book came out called UFO/Flying Saucers, issue #2 by Gold Key Comics. It illustrated UFOs on the moon and showed a field of obelisks. A narration by a man reporting the comic book illustration depicted him as having blood-red eyes, a typical demonic attribute.

In 1958 another comic book came out that looked similar to the face on Mars. "The actual face on Mars was photographed in 1976." How are we getting advanced information; is it through time travel, remote viewing or is it something else? The book, "The Law of One: Book 1, The RA Material by RA, claims he is a humble messenger of the Law of One, a positive entity that helped the Atlanteans and the Egyptians claiming that their messages got distorted and, as a consequence, they withdrew. They came back later through intuitive channelers. The rank and file of the Secret Space Program were told that the book was Luciferian, despite this the "brass" were told to read it. According to the book, the ETs taught that the only thing that exists in the universe is consciousness which would mean that there is only one consciousness however the one consciousness dispensed freewill creating multiplicity thereby creating Karma. It would seem that there are plans in the works to change this. Transhumanism seems to fit the bill.

Talk of companies in California and in the Denver, Colorado area were said to be beyond "Black". Work is being done on electrogravitics, Scaler technology, and etc. and their thoughts are that those in Congress and in the military that approve Black Budgets aren't even aware that there is a deeper "black". These projects have been taken off-line and are funded by some other mechanism.

CHAPTER 17

Here Today but Gone Tomorrow

Sergeant Clifford Stone served 22.5 years in the U.S. Army. During his tenure he was asked to serve as both the official and unofficial UFO consultant in his areas of assignment. He ascertained that our government knew more about UFOs than it's willing to tell. There were technologies in which an intelligence was involved and, to a degree, they were carrying on a dialogue with that intelligence. The sergeant said we're making every effort to incorporate their technology into ours. Their cover story was to be that this is in the interest of national security and, as part of the cover, they were to run a deception program. The program had a complete disregard for the individual witnesses and their families. On the contrary, Sergeant Stone believed that no government program has the right to destroy the lives of those that it is to serve. The government has a moral obligation to UFO witnesses, the real victims of the UFO phenomenon. They needed to expose this policy once and for all and to deliver the truth that we are not alone in the universe.

Ufology is moving toward understanding and disclosing the complexities of underground base activities, covert projects such as super soldier recruitment/induction, (their willingness or coerced cooperation), the secret space program, high-strangeness covert projects (time travel), the reverse engineering program, the applied ET technology program, the scientific study of consciousness, ET interface technology (currently being applied to corporate and military technology and, indicating by its name, that this technology has a consciousness), and psi based technology, (the study of both psychic and paranormal phenomena which includes telepathy, precognition, clairvoyance, psychokinesis, near-death experiences, reincarnation, apparitional experiences, and mental development). They found that when they comingled a psychic to technology <u>a connection was made.</u>

From abductee accounts, those of their witnesses, as well as from their case's physical evidence, researchers have amassed the following information that have surrounded the post abductee phenomenon:

- Being under surveillance, followed home or to their workplace.
- Black helicopter surveillance or harassment.
- Abductees have the ability to communicate psychically with ETs.
- The abductee experiences sightings or is in contact before an abduction.
- May have psychic contact before an abduction.
- Abductions run in families or are a past-life carryover.
- Threats are made to their family or friends if they communicate their experience.
- Their phones may experience electronic interruptions, convey harassment, or there may be intimidating or even threatening phone calls.
- E-mail and or regular mail are tampered with or there may be computer hacking involved.
- Warnings through direct face-to-face contact with "the men-in-black" or there may be men in suits or just a person in a shirt and shorts.
- They may experience illegal break-ins into their homes and property.
- In underground bases, witnesses have disclosed seeing implants either removed or being implanted by humans and seeing Reptilians with the MILABs in underground

bases. If humans have picked up the abductee, they may supplant the alien implant with one of their own.

- ETs abducting humans are accompanied by the MILAB standing by or, at other times, abductees are being handed over to humans who take it from there.
- The military has taken people both with and without an ET's presence.
- They utilize mind control procedures in which drugs are administered along with invoking fear, intimidation, and hypnosis.
- In-depth interrogation/debriefing procedures are used and at times will include physical abuse (being battered).
- Medical, genetic procedures, exploratory surgery, removal of plausible alien fetuses, and possible cloning experiments have been reported. There is an interest in genetic material while females ovulate.
- There is a testing for and demonstrations of psychic abilities.
- Telepathy and empathy are essential for understanding communication beyond the third dimension. The ET child has no interest who its father is.
- Parents are tested if they can interact with the hybrid.
- The human component is more stable than the ET component (reference what I wrote on the double DNA strand). That should tell you something.
- Involvement by intelligence community "insiders" and "minders" into the personal life of the abductee who became suddenly involved in the abductee's life through what appear to have been seemingly normal situation(s).
- The military has been known to orchestrate relationships. One of the reasons this is done is to take a person off of their physical and or their spiritual life's intended path.
- Vibrational energy has been taken from one to be given to another to make mating desirous to someone other than would have normally been chosen.

- Being recruited into covert programs unwillingly or unconsciously or willingly and consciously.

For the hybrids additional effects may include:

- Following the hybrid on their soul resonance e.g. great grandfather was in the Nazi party, a great aunt was a psychic, or there was clairvoyance in the mother's bloodline and that of being born in a military hospital.

  What is found in their blood type may indicate a superhero capability which is another reason why they may have been chosen to be chipped. Chipping allows for them to have been made into a virtual receiver. Once chipped this host/human receiver is capable of transmitting their capabilities in a positive or a destructive way given the signal that has been transmitted to them. The massive output of their human electromagnetic energy either natural or enhanced creates portholes into other dimensions. In part, it is the gene pool of the selected individual that has the capability to traverse dimensions which, in part is why those individuals' genes are being taken and replicated.

- They are chosen for their mental, physical, and or psychic abilities. Telepathy and empathy are essential for understanding communication beyond the third dimension. These conditions must be met if bypassing an occult initiation process.

The MILAB want the psychic's mental capabilities for their exclusive use and are attempting to reverse engineer the abductee developing within themselves the abductee's PSI development. The abductees have not been found to be "yes" people. Perhaps this is because many of them additionally may be sensitives who are aware, even at a subconscious level, the implications of saying "yes" which would account for so many of them having been taken by force.

Reverse engineering an abductee is about reverse engineering personnel. It is speculated that PSI abductees will be used in a later scenario and will have their mental capabilities melded with alien technology. Hence thoughts of the reported "living" ships come into my mind and the plausibility of the psychic living into eternity entombed in its new body, a craft. An insider said that the only thing keeping us from flying these back-engineered craft as intended is a psychic's mental hookup which will enable us to maneuver the craft as the aliens do.

I recently spoke with an occultist (secret knowledge) who himself has done extensive research. In his opinion, it is "the men-in-blacks'" job to conceal the dark, occult nature, and methods of operation employed by the Greys (servants of the Reptilians). From what I have found and experienced I agreed with him 100%. Others in the Ufology field have said that those associated with Ufology have, over time, become darker and darker. Their personal lives have come to be in tatters. I've noticed that when this darkness starts to takeover, it usually starts with sexual overtones and adulterous fancy.

If or when the potential abductee is seen as having the necessary training, willing or not they are inducted into the PSI or super soldier programs or into technology development.

> *In Chapter 8, I photographed my fluorescent markings after I had what I thought was a dream. In the pseudo dream, I was given a brief physical put into a uniform with a dark colour and yellow on it with a stylized "A" or what looked similar to a stylized "A" along with some other things around it appearing less significant than the "A" where a left pocket would have been. I believe that the yellow signified the PSI program. I didn't write much about it in that chapter.*

Through the employment of memory suppression techniques, seemingly more people are being inducted against their will. Covert-ops personnel obtain both technical and operational information from abductees. Special attention is paid to their genetics because they need a hybrid person to operate a hybrid technology which implies that hybrids are among us and the military is seeking them out.

If the outcome(s) of abductee's disclosures aren't seen as positive, if they are being used in a power play or are in some way are considered a profitable gain, their disclosure(s) could result in very negative, personal consequences that may result in their persecution. As a result of their disclosures, securing "rights" for them is being considered.

The U.S. Government and ETs

In the Exodus account, what was in the sky leading Moses to the promised land? Could it be that when Alijah was taken up into a chariot of fire that it was actually a UFO/abduction event, and what was the wheel within a wheel occurrence? What if these were actually UFO accounts in the bible?

John Keel disclosed many strange anomalies; among them he reported that since the 1940's there have been skyquakes in the Northeast. An explanation couldn't be found for the quake's explosion-like sounds. These reported sounds were in Native American legends going way back.

There was one particular hilltop that John would sit on while looking out onto the Ohio River watching the lights in the sky interact with lights shot up into the sky from the cargo boats. When John flashed Morris Code, they would do the same with him.

There was a worldwide epidemic of these lights in 1964-1968; the New York Times posted front page stories about them. People were getting burned from being near the lights because they released an energy. Other witnesses reported that they thought the lights were alive because they responded accordingly. These anomalies have come together in pivotal years. For example, the folks in India had no idea the same occurrences were happening in

China and the people in China had no idea that they were happening in India. Thus, these occurrences gave rise to a new age.

It is John's belief that the witnesses don't see what he/she claims they do because the reality may be, that a thought is being projected into the witness's mind. Consequently, the witness really isn't seeing what is actually there, instead, they are seeing what the projection/object or being wants the witness to see.

Around 2,500 years ago in Persia (Iraq/Sumer, part of the core of Persia), a man named Zoroaster talked to an entity named Mazda and from that he derived the concept of Devils and Angels which became the foundation for the Christian and Judaic religions.

1848 was another pivotal year. Carl Marx brought Communism to the forefront; there were scores of political assassinations and there were fifty revolutions. The Fox sisters heard rapping in their walls and founded spiritualism which spread all over the country. In 1968 there was a major flying saucer wave. Other waves of this nature were in the years 1973 and 1975. In 1975, a superfluity of abductions were reported as well as Bigfoot and sea serpent sightings. The press diverted its attention away from UFOs at the onset of the war.

The Majestic 12 were formed through a special, classified, presidential order on September 24, 1947, via Project "Signal" (an alleged deal between the U.S. government and extraterrestrials). Their purpose was to gather information on ETs and UFOs while attempting to keep this entirely away from unfriendly powers and the American public.

They were aware that four groups of ETs were visiting earth and that one group looked nearly identical to us. The military was especially bothered by this because they knew that one of the ETs in that group could pose as the president of the United States. This occurred at a time when many of the military had some misgivings about the occupants in the White House.

In 1961 a UFO study was initiated which included life-altering, firsthand reports on UFOs. From information gleaned in 1976, the military concluded aliens might be multidimensional in their source. The aliens demonstrated time and time again that they could manipulate matter and time and that <u>a process is underway</u>. At the time there were many new scientists talking about multiple dimensions, among them was a brilliant young professor in New York that wrote a book on hyperspace. A part of the text's contents mentioned ten separate dimensions that come and go into and out of our reality. Hence this is the likelihood of what is meant by a society said to occupy inner earth.

Disagreements popped up regarding how communication with the ETs first began however, once it had, it's uncertain if the EBEs either couldn't speak our language or that they refused to. As a consequence, telepaths were tasked (telepaths have been recruited as far back as the 1950s as far as we know) to gather the information that was required James V. Forrestal, Secretary of Defense under Harry Truman was the alleged mastermind behind MJ12. Once MJ12 had been created it expanded its telepathy mandate well beyond what Forrestal may have intended. He plunged to his death from a hospital window believing people had "a right know". While at the time he was being treated for depression, others thought his alleged suicide may have been the workings of MJ12.

It is suspected that the EBEs (artificial intelligence) waited until humanity developed to a certain point so that they could engineer direct encounters. They brought humanity a false hope in a guise to help us at a time when a small percentage of their "Trojan Horse" crashes had occurred.

Their technology is directed toward developing a "network" beaming AI signals via satellites across the Earth, into computers, and into our power grids. The ETs are said to have vast interstellar and galactic relay points which act like a wireless network broadcasting in all directions. At one time I suggested that the energy coming out of the Great Pyramid was intercepted at a relay point.

Deceptive and clever, they are known to reach out through telepathy and use the "trickster" alleging it is a god, a ploy to gain our trust. They are a living technology with an agenda, are negative and evil, and are in opposition to our interests and welfare. Once we have served their purpose, they will get rid of each and every one of us that hasn't been converted via Nano Tech (Black Goo) into one of them.

It is interesting to note that in an interview with a Grey, the Grey said, "you are us". With that said, if we refuse to be integrated with AI then we change our path and our history and, as a consequence, we eliminate the Grey we are intended to become; they cease to exist. If I was a Grey, I'd do my best to see that this doesn't happen.

The Greys are ancient and are said to be spread out like a plaque across multiple galaxies. "According to "Allied ET Documented History" AI's have taken over, ruled, and destroyed ET societies, planets, and entire solar systems. They are seen as an extreme and present danger to both other ET's and to humans".

At twenty-six years of age, Colonel Corso was the head of intelligence in Rome (CIC before the CIA). In a 1997 interview, he discussed contact and also his position as a missile commander at White Sands Missile Range. He was told to shut down the radar at certain times of the day but, realizing that they were bringing down unidentified craft, he ceased to listen to what he was told. One day, while he was flying over the area that he was in charge of he saw a craft, landed his plane then took a jeep over to it at which time the craft was alternating between appearing and disappearing.

A series of secret research projects within the Montauk Project were conducted at Montauk Airforce Base. These were an extension of the infamous Philadelphia Experiment (Rainbow Project) which was an experiment warping time and space It made a Navy ship, the USS Eldridge, become invisible to radar and also in its time/

space continuum. The Institute for Advanced Study at Princeton showed that earlier the project had a minor success through the work of Nicola Tesla and others. The late astronomer MK Jessup, the first individual to reveal the details of the Philadelphia experiment, passed away in 1959 and, like James V. Forrestal, he died from a *mysterious so-called, suicide.*

The Navy realized the project had a tactical application. On August 12, 1943, the Eldridge was specifically built for this project and was outfitted with burgeoning technology. Duncan Cameron was on board when the ship became invisible to radar before it became physically invisible until it disappeared entirely. A couple of the crew thought the party was getting a tad too rough so they jumped ship only to find themselves in the same vortex that the ship was caught up into. They found themselves coming out of a porthole in 1983 on the same date having gone back and forth in time a number of times. The ships deck logs have gone missing from August through December of 1943. When the generators for the project onboard were smashed, the rainbow over the ship stopped and the Eldridge returned to her harbor. A piece of the Montauk underground was said to have been floating in the air and this too, allegedly, returned to its rightful place at that time. In the aftermath people were found aimlessly walking on deck. Their minds were destroyed through the process while others had some of their body parts integrated into the ship's metal. The deck logs of the S.S. Andrew Furuseth, a ship that was sailing by chance near the Eldridge at the time of the experiment, were destroyed by executive order.

The project was relaunched in 1948 and its equipment was sent to Los Alamos. They made an effort to downsize the equipment which apparently met with success because it is now said that this technology is used on the Stealth Bomber which can attain full radar and physical invisibility.

Checking to see if what he saw was real, he threw a cactus under the craft and watched it being crushed. To the left of the craft was something that looked like a cave. Coming out of it, he saw what he thought was an extraordinary Grey (suggesting that he has seen them before or is aware of descriptions of them). What made this Grey extraordinary was that it was wearing a silvery helmet with a red stone in the middle forehead area of the helmet (this is likely where the third eye concept has come from). The stone in the center of the forehead is believed to have enabled the being to interface telepathically with its craft such as the plausible intended use of psychics interfacing with an alien flying technology. Corsco asked the Grey if it was a friend or a foe; it replied "neither". Thoughts of the alien as a self-serving being come into my mind as well as it has to others.

> *Alien reproduction vehicles were created through the use of channeling via an unknown alien source which was called alien technology by the Nazi's. Torsion Fields were created via Plasma Electric Fields. These same aliens directed the manufacture of the Veda's mentioned in ancient Indian texts. Those doing the channeling drew the faces of those they channeled which were similar to what we have come to know as the Greys years before a Grey was described at Roswell or in any known abduction scenario.*
>
> *In the beginning ARVs were used because at the time they weren't able to back engineer the EBEs crafts. The ARV's were simple and used mercury and copper counter rotating plates subjecting their pilots and anyone near the craft to a harsh field.*

A high-ranking military attaché with CIA connections stated, when it comes to the puzzle of the true nature of UFOs, the UFO phenomenon has three separate but related aspects:

1. It produces real material-world events, which are detectable by radar that may sometimes leave behind physical traces.
2. It's a psychic phenomenon that profoundly alters the consciousness of those exposed to it.

3. It is surrounded by deception activities mimicking it that are produced by human groups. We tend to consider these elements as mutually exclusive, but they're not; all three are explainable by demonic activity and invocation."

From "Foo Fighters" dogging our fastest planes in WWI and WWII, to the battalions of well-armed soldiers who walked into a strange ground-level cloud cover never to be seen again, global conflict seems to bring out the most hostile manifestations of UFOs. From time to time America's bravest have been seen marching into oblivion. Many top-secret aerial skirmishes have victimized pilots and passengers. Planes have "gone down" without a trace, and hundreds have been killed. There have been terrifying incidents of flaming destructions that have incinerated individuals or rendered them helpless. In one case UFOs left a military fort and its sentries smoldering, while entire coastal towns in Brazil have been "burned out," by what the locals have called chupa-chupas. Complete towns have disappeared in association with UFOs, while unsuspecting individuals have walked off wilderness trails in front of onlookers only to slip into a parallel universe inhabited by hobgoblins, men-in-black, and other cross-dimensional terrors declared the late Dr. James McDonald, a respected physicist.

According to Colonel Philip Corso, a covert government group was assembled under the leadership of Admiral Roscoe H. Hillenkoetter. Its tasks were to collect all off-planet technology information. A possible relationship has been found between Corso and MJ-12 and it is said to be in his official military records.

As the Chief of Research and Development, Corso ended up with the Roswell artifacts in his possession. Realizing the artifacts were important and, in an effort to understand what they had, they pushed them forward with the money they had. Employing what appears to be a child-like trust, they gave them out to industry with a single string attached. The string was that once the functions of the artifacts were determined and whatever else came out as a result, they were to be given back to the Army so that they could maintain a competitive edge. Corso alleged, that once determined, what was learned from the artifacts should be given to the people which, in my mind, doesn't seem to have been one of their strings as only one string, a military advantage, seems to have been their singular objective. It was the only thing mentioned at the time. The two directives (a military advantage and give to the people) are an oxymoron. They are completely nonsensical so had the wrong person been put into the right position or had the right person been put into the right position?

Reverse engineering the artifacts found at the crash near Roswell indirectly led to the development of accelerated particle beam devices, fiber optics, lasers, integrated circuit chips, and Kevlar material. Corso also claimed that the Strategic Defense Initiative (SDI), or "Star Wars", was meant to achieve the destructive capacity of electronic guidance systems for incoming enemy warheads, as well as disabling enemy spacecraft which included those of an extraterrestrial origin.

The MJ12 Operations' Manual of 1994 detailed the detainment of EBEs (extraterrestrial, biological entities) by whatever means necessary including their removal to a "secure" location as soon as possible once they were recovered. Although it was preferable to maintain the wellbeing of any entity, its loss of life was considered acceptable as long as the conditions or delays involved in preserving its wellbeing didn't compromise the security of the operation.

A retired Navy Petty Officer, a First-Class Flight Engineer that was now 61 years of age asked to be called Brian. Brian retired after 20 years of service in 1997. He was never asked to sign a "nondisclosure statement". He received an Antarctic service medal that was awarded to him on November 20, 1984. He has flown over the South Pole over 300 times.

He reported that his C130 crew encountered high-strangeness near an air testing station in a no-fly-zone. While in flight they saw an alleged entrance to a rumored science and ET collaboration research base under the ice. At a camp near Marie Byrd Land, twelve scientists disappeared for two weeks. When they reappeared,

Bryan's flight received orders to pick them up. Brian reported that the scientists would not talk and that their facial expressions indicated fear. Brian and his crew were told not to talk about it and were told that they did not see the ice-hole with its ramp leading down into it. The hole was approximately 138-360 feet across.

I stayed up late one particular night using Google Earth to scan Antarctica and saw a huge hole in the ice and snow and what looked like a line of vehicle tracks leading to it. Tired, I didn't want to stay up any longer thinking I could make a copy of what I saw later. About one week later I thought I'd go back and print what I saw but found the image had been edited out. On 08/15/2019 I took another look at Antarctica and saw pictures taken of large squares of snow that were overlaid onto other areas. The snow-patched pictures were deliberately put there to cover something up.

In his story, Brian confirmed that there was a line of tracks going out to the site. Back at their base, a scientist started talking about what was going on at the sampling station and other crew members said they were going out to talk to the non-human visitors having intimated that a human and alien corroboration was occurring.

Nearly one decade later, a new camp was installed for the National Science Foundation's scientists. They had enough supplies for at least one month. Communications were lost with the scientists for two days. The flight crew left to check on the camp but saw no movement from the air. When their plane taxied up to the camp, they found no one despite the fact that they accounted for all of their vehicles. Their radio was in working order and, at the time no tracks were seen leaving the camp. They went back to their base and filed a report. One week later the scientists called in and were waiting to be picked up long before their allotted time slot was up. All of their equipment was packed; the scientists moved as quickly as possible boarding the aircraft. For their entire return trip, they dawned paranoid expressions and didn't speak a single word even if it meant getting food or drink from the crew. It was later assessed that they may have had something similar to PTSD. The returning crew were directed to forget what they had done and to deny that they had picked up any scientists.

> *After visiting Antarctica Buzz Aldrin said he saw the face of evil. If it is as he says… do we want to come into contact with an evil presence? Brian is completely convinced that non-humans are currently working on this planet.*

The MJ12 Operations' Manual document's directive stated: Our military and government wanted weapon, propulsion, and metallurgy technologies. The ET's, on the other hand, wanted our genetic material. It appears as though they were given carte blanche to access to our genetic material and, in exchange, the military was given a number of flying saucers.

> *In the pursuit of monsters, governments themselves have become monsters. Rather than those horrific creatures portrayed in a science fiction movie these are monsters with human faces wearing crisp uniforms marching in close adherence to and emulating the actions of others. Because they appear to be so banal, government monsters aren't recognized until it's too late.*
>
> *In the quest for the acquisition of greater wealth, technological advances, scientific experimentation, and global conquest our government has unleashed untold horrors upon the world which are all packaged in the guise of "the greater good". When the government is involved there is no greater good. There is only greed for money and power. With the continued onslaught of public spectacles coming out of Washington, DC, the average public person has become so distracted that they are altogether oblivious to the goings-on of grisly experiments, barbaric behavior, and inhumane conditions.*

One of the artifacts given to Corso from Roswell was a lens, a night screening device that Grey's used. We ended up replicating it and used it Vietnam. Now that the populations' genetic material was and is still being collected, literally becoming a commodity, the dark subversive elite have been given new technology for their weapons leading toward the elimination of or the thinning of all human life. Is this leading somewhere; you bet!

In addition to accessing our genetic material, the EBEs were also given separate control of a base near Area 51. Bob Lazar stated that the EBEs said they generated some sort of a field at this base claiming it would set off the ammo our military carried on them. Interestingly enough, when on the EBEs delegated base, all of the humans involved that were on that base died of a head wound. The question I have is, is how could a firearm at their waist end up mortally wounding all of them in their heads?

Regarding the ongoing pedophilia involvement of Washington's lack-luster, pseudo elites, it is important that I bring up the following. There have been over eighty UFO events over the White House in 1952. In 2002, a UFO landed on the White House roof; its image was captured on 35mm film. In an account of "Covert Encounters Over Washington D.C," the report described UFO and extraterrestrial contact from 1850 through 2011 at our nations' capitol.

> *Symbolism has played a large role throughout the ages and stages of human development; in essence it is a language and thus it is a form of communication. "From "secret societies" like the Masons, Illuminati, major multinational corporations, governmental organizations, and financial institutions, intriguing symbolism has always been used." Within the military-industrial complex, energy, and health industries, occult symbolism on patches and etc. continue to be used. It is estimated that 80% of our military is involved in the occult whether on a conscious or subconscious level. In an interview I conducted, I have found that near Area 51 there is an incredulous amount of Satanic activity that continues to go back into their hills. A lack of participatory awareness does not constitute passive or inert participation. "Who is responsible for these patches; how do they come into being, and what has been their inspiration?"*

If you want to understand what is really going on, on our planet and the secrecy behind it, a look needs to be taken at our Military Industrial Complex. One of eight Air Force Satellite remote tracking stations, the 23rd Space Operations Squadron U.S. Air Force patch, shows a hooded, beady-eyed being hunched over the earth. Its unidentifiable face is hidden in the shadows of its hood. It overshadows the world; its gaze is focused on Africa and Europe. To its right is a triangular craft and to its left is a four-pointed star. The military has always had some type of Reptilian attribute on their patches and symbols. At the bottom of the badge, it says, "Semper Vigilans" meaning always vigilant. Does this mean that the being observing earth is always watching and what of the Black Knight satellite?

A second patch belonging to the U.S. Air Forces' 509th Bomb Wing Crew who flew the B-2 stealth bomber test flights in the late 1940s and early '50s. has an image on it that looks like a Grey alien is tightly grasping a Stealth Bomber as if it was a toy. The upper part of the patch reads "to serve man" and the bottom reads Gustatus Similis Pullus which translates into "tastes like chicken". Again, this is another reference referring to the consumption of man.

The third patch I'm mentioning is the patch for NRO's load that was launched aboard a United Launch Alliance Delta IV. This was the second in a series of six launches for the NRO's 50th anniversary. It is a triangular patch with a pyramid in the background. Superimposed onto that pyramid is a large eye. Underneath the pyramid are the Roman numerals "32" which have a numerical value of five (the Pentagon has five sides as does the pentacle). I'm sure many of you are familiar with this pyramid and eye-like logo. We see it everywhere, and on major corporations and financial institutions on the planet. However, this eye has a very rounded shape and is shaped like the R-Complex, the Reptilian part of our brains. The eye on the one-dollar bill is shaped differently, however its meaning may be the same.

The connection seen through symbolism in major corporations belongs to the same bloodlines. The symbolism connecting all major ruling facets of our world are pyramids and all-seeing eyes. Reptilian references are a common trend throughout modern-day times as well as in ancient history. The Air Force does not hide their patches however the information on their design's inspirations can't be found.

In the nonfiction book, "Terminate with Extreme Prejudice", there was a description of an island in Michigan where there was a high incidence of UFO sightings near the great lakes. Because of these sightings a law enforcement officer was sent there to surveil why children from prominent families were going missing. From his investigation, he gleaned that many things were being run by a high-level Masonic group, some of which were involved in Satanic practices. While preparing to do his surveillance, he was told that no matter what he saw he was not to engage. Allegedly he recorded some of the known, missing children being brought there whereupon a satanic ritual was conducted using the children in which drugs, chanting, sex, and symbols were employed. It was nearly dawn when a spacecraft showed up taking the children away. He took his recording equipment back to the police station when he was finished. The only thing they found on his recordings was "white noise" (which is typical at true UFO sightings). Once finding this out, another officer said that he was going to look into it however before he could, he was found murdered. After the intended follow-up officer's death, the officer that did the initial investigation ran for his life; from then on, his life was made to be continuously miserable.

Many in secret societies believe that they are in the same bloodline as these unclean entities. Alister Crowley's magickal motto was: "of royal blood". I thought it interesting that these entities, as well as some in the inner circle of Masons both, perform Luciferic acts. Note that it has been described that the entities arrived in UFOs and, according to the first paragraph, the noun "entities" is synonymous with what was written as "extraterrestrials"; both are one and are interchangeable. As it turned out, it was determined that the children's innocence was sacrificed as an offering to those entities/extraterrestrials serving the Luciferian agenda.

As few would imagine, there are credible ties to the Kennedys and werewolves. In an odd event, John Kennedy and Attorney General Robert Kennedy were in a hellish, Southeastern part of Wisconsin in the same local of a cryptid that resembled a traditional werewolf. However, we first need to visit what was happing with Joseph and Rose Kennedy in 1941. Joe Jr. and Jack Kennedy both joined the U.S. military while Kathleen took a job at the Washington Times-Herald. During this time the Kennedy clan was trying to deal with the tragic problem of Joseph Senior's trying to cure his daughter Rosemary's learning and behavioral disabilities. Rosemary was given a newfangled surgery, lobotomizing her brain's frontal lobe which made her problem worse. She was institutionalized at St. Coletta, a school for Exceptional Children. A former security guard at the school kept the truth from the Kennedy's that a furry, upright, man-size predator was stalking the school's grounds.

Initially, the pastoral setting of St. Coletta may have appeared to have been a safe place to serve as a security guard. Mark surveilled its 174-acre grounds that were embellished with orchards, gardens, and religious statues. Long before St. Coletta had been established, others previously groomed the grounds for what they called sacred religious purposes. The site was dotted with Native American burial mounds. St. Coletta is five or six miles Southeast of Astalan State Park which is famous for its mysterious flat-topped, earthen <u>pyramids</u>.

Mark Schaclkelman, the guard, had a midnight encounter with the creature in 1936 which wasn't made public until nearly six decades later. The watchman's attention was drawn behind the main building where he watched a man-sized creature covered in dark fur digging into a mound around midnight having left large claw marks into it in sets of three. It stood six feet tall and smelled of rotting meat. It appeared to be a mix of candid, primate, and human which screams of genetic engineering or it may be another creation, created through the twisted terrors of the human mind. It was said that its side profile resembled that of Anubis, the Egyptian jackal-headed god of the dead. Schackelman saw its powerful arms that ended in "hands." Its thumbs and pinky fingers were significantly shorter than its middle three digits.

Muscoda is relatively close to St. Coletta and is sandwiched between two wildlife units and hilly, wooded farms. To its north, across the river, lay a cluster of ancient mounds that included a bird-shaped effigy with a wingspan of roughly one-quarter of one mile. The Muscoda area possesses all of the hallmark associations of a creature-sighting hotspot between wildlife habitat, Indian mounds, and water. The Wisconsin River is especially significant to the state's native peoples who believe it was carved by a great spirit <u>serpent.</u> He slithered from the Mississippi to the Great Lakes (a place of frequent USO sightings) into the area of the state where it was reported that the missing children were seen whereupon a satanic ritual was conducted on them and UFOs were reported to have picked them up at Dawn. "Perhaps the great serpent left a few furry pets along the way".

Liz Crokin is an investigative journalist and a champion for children. She has dedicated her career in her efforts to expose leading entertainment, the pedophile ring of the pseudo elites, business leaders, and the church clergy (who perform satanic rituals). She asserts that she has found, which she feels would prove that Pizzagate is real and is occurring.

A video was found on the Dark Web featuring Hillary Clinton and Huma Abedin. The video is considered the Rosetta Stone connecting Washington senior politicians to the Luciferian agenda via their sexual act with an underage girl. The video was said to be so sickening that it made senior police officers' vomit and cry. It was gut-wrenchingly unforgettable and, like most truth, the video has been removed. A Greek saying states: "a fish rots from its head downward". Since I have been investigating high strangeness, I have had to learn many things outside of my comfort zone into what may be called the "fringe'.

In child exploitation, **Fear** is the tool of choice. It's the underpinning theme whether it is a consequence of an action or whether **FEAR** is intentionally induced as part of that action. During the course of a fear-inducing event, oftentimes, incredible knowledge is relayed to the recipient or the initiators of these interactions. It is as though there is some unknown rule of reciprocity or perhaps it may be a cosmic rule that something has to be given in order to take something. The issue that I want you to understand at this time is the importance the role of inducing **FEAR** may play in alien and or the ultra-terrestrial experience.

> In a development that calls to mind both vampire lore and stories of bathing in blood, "young blood" appears to be able to rejuvenate ageing brains. Below is an article explaining why **Fear** may be part of the alien abduction process and in today's child/youth abduction scenarios.
>
> In an article by Tony Wyss-Coray (Stanford University) in 2014, he and other researchers discovered that infusions of blood from young mice reversed cognitive and neurological impairments seen in old mice. This procedure allowed two mice, a young and an old, to share the same circulatory system (known as Parabiosis). For their study, they sutured young and old mice together finding that the old mice that were conjoined to their youthful counterparts showed changes in their gene activity and brain region (the hippocampus) as well as having increased neural connections and enhanced "synaptic plasticity" (the mechanism believed to underlie learning and memory). An additional study was published in "Nature" by Wyss-Coray and his colleagues. They went even further to show that plasma from human umbilical cords and young adults also had beneficial

effects. It is believed that this has been a successful process because it lengthened their telomeres (Ambrosia Plasma). Given that we are still discovering incredible and at times, ill-used technology from ancient times, this may be an indicator why there may have been bloodletting sacrifices in those times.

Receiving blood from someone younger is an outpatient procedure and takes about two hours to perform. A one-liter treatment goes for $8,000 and a two-liter treatment is $12,000. The company, Ambrosia, (young blood) solicits modern vampirism by openly raising money to give young blood to the aged. Information regarding this can be found in the following video: https://youtu.be/BKOlh6im1oU

After having experienced utter, intense, immeasurable fear, a young abductee will make Adrenochrome in their bloodstream. Adrenochrome provides better health, increased vivacity, a high like no other without ill effects, and a host of other smaller effects. Combine these with a substantial euphoria and they will have created a significant demand for" young blood".

Despite these studies, one has to consider the grotesque, sickening photos where these children, usually under the age of 15 are kept naked and chained in a windowless room, (sometimes the size of a football stadium) in what is called a farm. While they're being tortured, their blood is drained simultaneously. There is no need to continue any further describing the actions these groups are taking.

I culled the following from an anonymous source: "On the far side of the table, almost too small to be seen but still unmistakable, was an iconic head of state; a recent one laughing as he reached for his syringe. There was something unusual about his hand. It wasn't normal, smaller, nor flesh colored as we are. His hand was "green" suggesting that he was either a Reptilian or a Reptilian hybrid.

184

> *When I joined my temple, as part of the initial initiation process, we were told not to get drunk nor to use drugs. The reason being is that when a person uses meth, marijuana, cocaine, or etc. it does something to their chakra system that allows them to be more easily manipulated, allowing possession to readily take place by an Archonic or demonic entity. British and American soldiers both used amphetamines allowing themselves to be hacked into by psycho-spiritual beings. Drugs, including those brought in by the military, are another means by which to program man.*
>
> *Ronald Reagan's speech given to the U.N. General Assembly in 1987 did little to dispel the notion that human and alien cooperation had come to an end. At the time it was also stated that they were a recognized threat. Perhaps now you may be starting to understand why the Pentagon is not talking about the full implications of disclosure.*

In 1952, the Director of Air Force Intelligence admitted to more than 300 cases of radar tracking; visual sightings were confirmed by radar. In the ensuing years, there have been at least 2,000 additional radar cases in the U.S. alone. Reports have come from expert operators in the Army, Navy, Air Force, Marine Corps, Coast Guard, Federal Aviation Agency, pilots, and the radar operators of almost all major airlines. The same situation exists in foreign countries. Not only has radar proved UFOs a reality, it has accurately recorded their high speeds, intricate maneuvers, precise UFO formations including their changing from one formation to another and other important data.

CHAPTER 19

The Unacknowledged Space Program

Until the U.S. Government provides actual, reproducible facts and the media publicly validates them, we won't know much and, even then, the information due to us will likely be managed. John Lenard Walson used a special telescope camera system he designed to zoom in and record large Starships in our Earth's orbit." Many of them appear as stars however, when they're zoomed in upon, they are seen as ships. Are these ships from our secret space program or are they from demon/aliens? Joe Jordan has proof that all aliens are demonic. Not just some, ALL of them.

Disclosure isn't likely to happen anytime soon because the U.S.G. has had a history of lock-downs since WWII. "In the past, when serious secrets were revealed in special Congressional hearings such as those relating to MK-Ultra, Iran Contra, radiation experiments involving humans, and the like, they have received little traction in the major mass media and thus were prevented from wide recognition among the populace. Before William Colby, the CIA director died he said that one way or another the CIA controlled every major newscaster and news outlet in the free world through a program called Operation Mockingbird.

It has become quite clear that with the emergence of "the powers that be," the secret shadow government, is largely due to American and British intel both of whom gained information from Nazi anti-gravity technology, crashed and recovered alien UFOs, and ET bodies recovered at the Roswell crash site along with two other sites in the American Southwest.

The visible U.S.G. (our elected officials) serve as our ceremonial government, however, the most senior senators and representatives, especially those heading intel committees know that most of the power lies within the Secret Shadow Government.

"The best available description of the Secret Shadow Government (S.S.G.) was assembled by Richard Boylan, Ph.D. http://www.bilderberg.org/secret.htm." For example, the newer multibillion-dollar police state of Homeland Security was set up under mysterious circumstances right after 911. It runs all American national security and intel. With the documentation that has been accumulated so far, it's questionable if 911 wasn't a planned demolition which had some very suspect circumstances leading to the intentional setup and the deliberate creation of the TSA. Recently TSA's director told Congress that it had no jurisdiction over his agency. If Congress has no jurisdiction over an agency it ushered into fruition, then who really runs Homeland Security? The shadow government runs it as well as the U.S. Space Command. As long as the S.S.G. keeps a complete lock-down on UFOs and their related technologies while exerting complete control over politicians and bureaucrats, it will remain impossible for Americans to have much say in how their country is run or how their money is spent.

At one time the leaders of the S.S.G. were outsmarted via an alleged treaty that was signed in 1954 by President Eisenhower at Holloman Air Force Base. Through their treachery, the entities seduced and compromised them using mind control techniques thus placing America under the control of an alien agenda? Some have claimed that the document was signed in 1953, others have said it was signed in 1956 while there are others that claim it was actually signed in 1947. In order to gain technology did the S.S.G. top officials align themselves with one group of aliens they thought were good in order to fight another that were exceedingly evil only to find out both were bad having compromised their integrity by forming conflicting coalitions?

As the story goes the supposed "good aliens" didn't abide by the treaty. Their lack of cooperation follows suit with the many inferences in this text that they are self-serving and therefore cannot be trusted. One of their recovered crashed craft had numerous human body parts in it that were the result of human dissections.

After careful consideration, it was decided that the best thing to do was to continue cooperating with the aliens in order to keep obtaining their high technology even though they technically violated the treaty. Using what they learned, they continued to work on making weapons that were capable of shooting down their anti-gravity craft in the hopes of defeating them. It is with extreme naivety that they assumed they could defeat them. The aliens would not have given us the level of technology needed to have put themselves into a vulnerable position. In this text, a way to defeat or control them is implied. What the government et alia has given them in trade to procure their technology is too high of a price and again, they have been duped if this has been the case. There is a rat in the cookie jar!

In the process of working with the aliens, it has been rumored that some of the S.S.G. controllers became victims of their advanced mind-control shifting their allegiance to the "dark side" having accepted the alien agenda. Others branched off to resurrect the U.S. Constitution and Bill of Rights exacting control away from the alien agenda. Their agenda however, isn't exclusively a lack of freedom and total control; these are the necessary precursors to their actual agenda.

According to the scientist, Thomas E. Bearden, traveling into the universe really isn't traveling into space, instead, it's a "flipping" into another space that may be only inches away; rather than traveling through space/time like a bullet, the time has been made to flip. If we're capable of controlling "flipping" we're able to flip from where we are into the fourth or fifth dimensions thereby literally jumping between galaxies. Another way many of us have already begun to travel through space is by having our bodies, (physical objects) dematerialize transitioning into a being of pure energy materializing once again when we have reached our destination. A comparison would be astral travel and the reported cases of being in two places simultaneously.

A vehicle capable of flipping time enables them to open up multiple dimensions in hyperspace and, by turning at a right angle, they would lose one dimension. Having lost one dimension, they would appear to be a light-form which has often been mistaken for something of a higher good. After having made three right angles, they would have lost all three dimensions and, once losing all three dimensions, they would have attained full dematerialization according to Bearden.

I've often wondered what the significance was, if any, regarding the four right angles on the Swastika however there is a correlation with the Nazi version of the Swastika and the "black sun" (a black energy). Although the Swastika is a symbol with many positive meanings it is also a symbol of esoteric and occult significance which comes from the idea of a hollow earth. The Nazis believed it could be accessed through the North or South Poles where portholes as said to exist. The earth may not be hollow but instead, a dimensional shift may happen there.

Thomas Bearden was able to prove his point when he took a photograph of the stars through a dematerializing spacecraft. Additionally, he was also able to prove it could be done mathematically.

A common sentiment shared between Jacques Vallee and John Keel when speaking about UFOs was that they believe there may be something extra-dimensional going on. In regard to the ETs visiting earth, they believe that a possible window to another dimension has opened up which is why there have been so many various sightings (e.g. Bigfoot). No one has caught Bigfoot as of yet; there is a possibility that it may be connected to our reality and to that of a parallel dimension(s). This would mean that the possibility exists that these entities operate at a different frequency. Are they or could they also be archetypal figures/beings created through our collective consciousness based on fears or subliminal functions of our psyche? For hundreds of years, people worldwide have reported encounters with monsters, fairies, demons, and cryptids. To this day those experiences persist.

> The medium, Maria Orsic, was the leader of a Nazi secret society, known as the Vril. It existed in the WWII era. After Maria received communication from extraterrestrials who had once lived in what is now <u>Sumer</u>, the Vril named themselves after the ancient Sumerian word "Vri-ll," which meant "God-like." Their society believed that they could use their telepathic abilities to communicate with otherworldly beings which gave the Nazis an advantage over their opponents.
>
> After having made contact with the extraterrestrials, Orsic transcribed the information they received into two different scripts. The first script was a secret German Templar language that she didn't personally understand and the second was an ancient language that historians commonly link to the Thule, a German occult group. "Most scholars are in agreement that these languages stem from Sumer where extraterrestrials once thrived." Once the information was translated into German, the Vril were shocked. The ancient race had given Orsic extremely detailed instructions for constructing a flying saucer.
>
> Among Nicola Tesla's manuscripts was a book called Occult Ether Physics: It described Tesla's ideal flying machine and the conspiracy to conceal it. According to

*Tesla, Ether fills all space and is <u>acted upon by a lifegiving</u> <u>force/</u>**Spark**<u>;</u> it is infinite in all worlds/dimensions. Once it nears the speed of light ether becomes ponderable matter. When the force subsides and its motion ceases this "matter" reverts back to its original form of Ether. It is <u>an</u> <u>infinite form of energy</u> that <u>man</u> or an alien can harness and can manipulate with the **Spark** of man.*

    William Lyne wrote about a conspiracy that dealt with the concealment of Tesla's ideal flying machine. Among those papers were numerous pages on anti-gravity in which he wrote about the latest devices that are capable of changing all known conceptions in physics. This would have changed everything we know in the "white world" about flight today. As we see more and more that this technology is being removed from mainstream knowledge; it lends to the proof that there is a breakaway civilization.

Captain Bill Uhouse spent ten years in the Marine Corps. Four of his working years were spent working with the Air Force as a civilian having taken a job at Wright Patterson Air Force Base doing flight testing. During this time, he was approached to work on a flying-disc simulator. It went into operation in the early '60s. The simulator was modeled after the craft that crashed in Kingman, Arizona, a craft that the aliens allegedly wanted to present to our government. The craft had its own interior gravitational field.

The human mind created perpetual distortions in flight. In order to handle the craft, the mind had to be trained to handle a ship that didn't have an outward view except through cameras in its turret area. It was anticipated that the craft would be easy to operate once the pilot understood what was going to happen to his/her body, knew what the instruments were, and where they were operating in space. The disc's design is too exacting and because it is, it couldn't be used as we use an airplane today. Its design had to be perfect and as such, nothing could have been added.

They were permitted to ask the EBE specific questions only on a "need to know basis". If the EBE was spoken to it would reply replicating the questioner's speech, reacting as though a trained parrot would. Most of the time the EBE couldn't understand their questions until they were first put onto paper and even then, they had difficulty.

The engineers needed to prove mathematically that the craft would fly. Initially, some of the calculations they were given were too difficult so the EBE helped them. During the interview, a picture of the craft was drawn. It was a black triangle with a light on each corner and one in its center. There are two or three 30-meter crafts in its center that have to meet the same specific design requirements that the discs do. It has been said that through downloaded information, during the last forty through sixty years or so, we have built around two or three dozen different crafts. The need for secrecy on these was compared to that of the first atomic bomb.

You may have asked yourselves why the comparison between the Greys, plausible others, and the atomic bomb. The bomb's electrons have a magnetic spin which

manipulates the nucleus releasing extremely destructive forces that penetrate through the earth into the abyss (the lower spirit world, the same world that is called inner earth, a world that came about as a result of the rebellions in heaven). The bomb's frequency penetrates the abyss and, as a consequence, the gates to the abyss/ Hell are now open.

In an interview between Joe Rogov (I hope I've spelled that correctly) and Tom De Longe: During the cold war, our military lived under the constant threat of nuclear war. Every single day we believed in the deepest part of our souls that nuclear war could happen at any time. Somewhere in those years, we found a life form.

Tom reminded his interviewer that the aliens (addressed as the visitors) turned our nuclear weapons on and readied them for launch. Just so Russia could pick up on that we were firing our missiles first the UFO's turned our missiles on just so the Russians could fire theirs first. Everything we did and every decision we made with that life-form was based on the "consciousness" we had in those bleak days. Regarding the matter, his contactee pointed a finger at his face and said "there are heroes in Russia and, under grave risk to themselves and to their country, they did not fire back.

"The significant problems we have cannot be solved at the same level of thinking with which we created them." - Albert Einstein

As posted earlier, this is an Archon/Reptilian. For some reason I can't get the entire image to print onto this page. Given how its neck is positioned I could see that it was sweeping down from the sky. Because it was flying this may have been a Draco Reptilian. I photographed this in Southern Oregon, an area that is believed to have a high radon (radiation) content.

It has been alleged that a secret space program was initiated in 1994; what if it was true? Having had ETs directing us, the program's proponents told us that it can take us through the solar system and beyond. Money isn't the only price that is being paid for the information that they are receiving. Their price tag is leaching out into the private sector, the comprehension of which belongs in a horror movie. Recently, President Trump directed the establishment of a U.S. force, one many believe already dominates space. Is there a threat and, if so, who leads this celestial fleet and is it being led against something? As the world prepares for a war in the heavens. Spiritual warfare is alive and well on this planet.

As many of us have, Richard Sauder began experiencing the paranormal in his early childhood through puzzling events leaving him thoroughly persuaded that there is more to the earth and to what humans' experience through their filters of consciousness and in their perceptions.

Dr. Richard's favorite research embraces underground and underwater bases and tunnels, electronic mind control, freedom technology, human prehistory, remote antiquity, alternative thought patterns, and etc. He began his underground and underwater bases and tunnels research in 1992 and has continued with it into the present. He has a B.A. in sociology, an M.A. in Latin American studies, an M.S. in forestry, a Ph.D. in political science, and is the author of three books. He is asking "what is the government hiding"? As he has put it, a brood of vipers (the deep state/the breakaway civilization) has set up its nest within the bowels of the U.S. Government, the military complex, and in associated alphabet agencies.

Darren Perks with the UK News reported that since 1980 there has been a secret space fleet which goes by the code name "Solar Warden". Since knowledge of this is largely unknown to the public the question is, is this subject too sensitive or is it that the consequences involved in achieving its disclosure are excessively problematic? Darren was able to speak to a NASA representative who confirmed that indeed this was their program. It was terminated by the President. It was not a joint program with the DOD (Department of Defense). The NASA representative informed him that he should direct his questioning toward the Johnson Space Center FOIA (Freedom of Information) manager. Eventually, Darren's request was run through a space-related directorate. The response delivered to Darren was that the program operated as classified under the U.S. Government and also under the United Nations' authority stating that there were many others that have tried very hard to find out the truth and have succeeded through leaked information or their asking questions and having government departments slip-up freely giving the information away. One notable contributor to this acquisition was Gary Mckinnon.

Mckinnon hacked into the computers of the U.S. Space Command several years ago and learned of the existence of "non-terrestrial officers", "fleet-to-fleet transfers", and a secret program called "Solar Warden". Gary was charged by the Bush Justice Department with having committed "the largest, military computer hack of all time".

Two Navy insiders, who chose to remain anonymous, released their testimony regarding a multinational coalition that has a secret space program with bases in Antarctica, the Moon, Mars, and even beyond our solar system. Because they chose to remain anonymous, pseudonyms were used in place of their names. In the official documents that were presented, it was learned that one of the confidants who was also an intelligence specialist was a U.S. Navy Seal who retired at the rank of Commander in the U.S. Marine Corps. He witnessed a large octagon (eight sides have represented a laboratory in the past e.g. the great pyramid) shaped structure buried 50 feet under the Beardmore Glacier, which extended deep down. The second confidant discussed covert activities that ran out of the 8th floor of the NSA Headquarters at Fort Meade, home of the U.S. Cybercommand, both of which are involved in running the space operations of a multinational alliance and the interstellar trade it conducts.

> *It is important to focus on the words interstellar trade as many have alleged, it involves human trafficking. There was also a treaty that was supposed to have been signed-in Antarctica. In an exchange for the technology, they traded their own females to be used as breeding stock. Let that sink in for a bit!*

He also disclosed that there is a base on the far side of the moon which is both above and below ground and it is used by a multinational alliance. He also stated that there is an operation going on the Moon and claimed that they are in the process of building a mothership. The statements expressed by the two men suggested that neither has actually visited the Moon base. They became aware of it through documentation, briefings, and a first-hand source they encountered during classified missions. On January 29, 1998, the International Space Station Intergovernmental Agreement was signed.

Has an elaborate demonic tapestry been woven over us with the pentagon's missing trillions of dollars? Fletcher Prouty was a colonel in the U.S. Air Force and was also a liaison officer during the height of the cold war between the U.S. military and the CIA. He played a key role in Operation Paperclip and brought Nazi technicians to the U.S. following WWII.

This photograph was taken at the National Atomic Testing Museum indicating collaborations

Richards asked Prouty about one of the underground installations in Warrington Virginia not far from Washington D.C. where the U.S. Army had two known training stations and where there are allegedly two more training stations. It was later found that these were not Army training facilities but were special access, CIA training facilities operating under the cover of the United States Army. Within the formal organization of the Pentagon, the CIA ran its own covert programs, having worn a variety of military branch uniforms in the process. There were admirals, colonels and etc. that had them as members none of which answered unto them. Included in this string of covert operations were equipment, raw resources, weapons, men, and money used for their clandestine projects. This accounted for the Pentagon's Inspectors' Generals, acknowledging that they had trillions of dollars flowing through their accounts that didn't require validation with any specificity.

It is believed that now, thirty years later, the NSA and the CIA are more integrated into the Pentagon than ever connecting them to underground bases and waterways many of which are still unknown. Because the projects have been compartmentalized, not all of those whom had top secret clearances were aware. Even then the "need to know" people who asked for additional information other than what they were told may have been singled out for "special attention".

Dr. John Pina Craven, a WWII veteran, got his Ph.D. in Oceanography. He was put in charge of the Navy's deep underwater project which was nearly four miles deep and was tasked with sending manned operators to crushing depths to do whatever they had to. It is unknown how deep they actually went. He would not discuss his deep-submergence using his pseudo rescue vehicles that had complex and unusual capabilities exceeding those of the space shuttle.

Richards ran across documents from a group at China Lake, California when he saw designed, manned, undersea bases housing multiple, large, military submarines that were kept in airlocks. Is the dark vile entity, the Deep State preparing to escape while we watch daily indicators edging us closer to a global disaster.

Please see the opening presentation of the Gotthard Tunnel (Cern)l: https://www.youtube.com/watch?v=TlG5WR *TeaY It will show you the darkness they're embracing under the tutelage of Satan at the site of the Hadron Collider.*

Project Paperclip seeded General Walter Dornberger and Wernher Von Braun into the Military Industrial Complex along with some others. Project Dynasoar (the 1950s and 60s) was to be the U.S. Air Force's space shuttle program. Before going to NASA, Neil Armstrong had been in the Dynasoar program.

Over the decades the U.S. military had four separate manned space programs which paralleled NASA in the course of training their own astronaut corps. Once this had been accomplished, they shut down their programs. It has been alleged that these were covers for the real secret space program. Emulating the wizard of Oz, NASA deflected attention away from what was really going on. An example of one of the operations was the X37B spaceplane which was sent up in orbit for one year. It is suspected that its classified information was apparently meant for the deep state's ears only. The fix is evidently in; the apparatus controlling the Pentagon is the same as that controlling the IRS (the collection arm of the Federal Reserve) which pays no taxes with one small exception.

Although the information coming forward will be managed, UFO disclosure will not come as a surprise to hardcore believers.

CHAPTER 20

God Rests in the Brain

For a long period of time faeries, aliens, et alia, seem to have acculturated themselves alongside humans, adapting their phenomenology to our cultural creeds, all-the-while maintaining their own specific, metaphysical identities keeping their presence persistently in our lives. "If prepared, we would set aside our automatic skepticism and the reductionism of our age spelling out the problem in a plain language finding ourselves contemplating the existence of highly intelligent, discarnate entities belonging to an order of creation fundamentally different from our own by whatever name we know them e.g. spirits, faeries, or aliens.

When tracing modern faeries et alia part of the problem is that the conditions of their appearances are not usually controllable so accounts of interactions with them tend to be anecdotal and unverifiable. If a mind is attempting to discern what is real or what is not that is less capable of critical thought or their knowledge base is left wanting, confusion creates indecision and therefore no action is taken.

They must have a definite, independent reality outside of the human brain yet some have become integrated into the brain's network either through initiation, drugs, (whether they be alcohol or some other substance) frequency or through the breeding program. Partly due to the exponential growth of alternative information which has been gained through the Internet in recent years, a new understanding of what aliens, faeries, and spirits are is beginning to emerge. Their presence throughout history is not the product of over-imaginative storytelling, but rather that they are deeply embedded within our collective consciousness, and are able to surface into consensus reality when certain conditions are met.

These beings operate in higher realms of existence/frequencies/dimensions and or operate in our own using an electromagnetic affect/frequency to manifest or to become invisible and, as such, they have the capability to alter their appearances through the manipulation of frequency. All that are considered ETs, the paranormal, or ultraterrestrials may not operate under the same conditions but many are. The creative power of the mind of man (being an electromagnetic being) makes this possible.

Belief is a psychological system (a force) defining each of us as a person which drives our humanness in and reverence for a supernatural power. Credo, ergo sum, "I believe, therefore, I am" and or it could also be said, I believe therefore I create. What we believe becomes our reality, shapes our perception(s) and hence the axiom "Perception is a reality"; it manifests and, likewise, what we believe becomes. If one worships a deity or creates one in their mind their thought (a form of energy) accumulates and eventually their thought acquires a life of its own and it becomes a reality. Are there as many different timelines, universes, entities or dimensions that would exist if there weren't minds and souls with consciousness creating them? Two examples are Mothman or Bigfoot that may have been created out of varying circumstances and for different reasons?

> As an offshoot of the Montauk project their psychic, Duncan Cameron, through alien technology, worked with a computer that could take human thoughts (the psychic's), which would be run through a computer then through a transmitter, and other equipment then would be fed into another human's brain (spirit/soul) and that human would act in accordance with the psychic's wishes. This was essentially a mind amplifier; it overrode the subject's defense mechanisms. The psychic was also able to visualize and create a full and complete physical reality

known as a virtual reality. Once the psychic's thought had gone through the system his thoughts created a thought-form into a physical reality. There were occurrences when the psychic would visualize a different time period and could make an object appear in that time period well before the transported object was even invented e.g. finding a digital camera on a table in the seventeenth century. They experimented with materializing objects around the base. Sometimes the created thought-form would appear within a timeframe rather than at a specific time which meant that time was being bent. By 1981 they had a working time tunnel. They realized the project was getting too scary when they could change the life of Christ if they wanted to. The employees working there said the Montauk project needed to crash so they asked Duncan to create a monster from his subconscious mind, a Bigfoot. Duncan started the process but when creating the thoughtform of the Bigfoot he hadn't made a connection with space or a time when he created it. The monster created from his subconscious became physical and real. It was angry, frightened, and violent; it started ripping things up. Attempting to end Bigfoot's rampage the transmitter's wires were cut but still, it continued. There were glowing masses and alternate realities going on in the building and all kinds of other wild stuff. It finally ended when the amplitrons were cut off.

In another example of the mind's ability to create (the **Spark***) and to bring the object intended to be created into physical reality is the Shapeshifter/Skinwalker. Most sources will say that the Skinwalker or Shapeshifter is a witch. If the shaman, or medicine person hurts another he or she has chosen to take the dark path while others will say that they take on other shapes for benign reasons like teaching. From some of those studying this phenomenon extensively, they have determined in most cases that the medicine person doesn't necessarily change shape physically but instead projects an apparition of personal energy called the astral double or calls forth a separate spirit form to surround the person, sort of a semi-tangible* *animal suit. They learn to create alternative appearances such as an upright wolf; an example might be Dogman. Earlier in this text, I've given examples of how I have shapeshifted either through my own ability or through something else.*

If our universe is a simulation, what mind(s) have created it or for that matter, what continues to amend it? The way things are digressing (some may call it progressing) a Skynet will likely be built. By definition, a Skynet is an artificial neural network-based conscious group mind and an artificial general intelligence system. Verily, this is "the Matrix". If it is suspected that we already live in one then this one is either being modified or it is being replaced. It has been said that tighter controls need to be placed over us and the mousetrap we're slated for is going high-tech. Obviously, we are on the cusp of finding out what our past and futures are as well as becoming aware of where we fall in the food chain. The makers of the mousetrap beholding to pure evil are on board with the technology coming forth.

As if the many universes are a note in a chord of music, Astrophysicists are questioning how many universes may exist beyond this one or how many reverberate from it which begs the question, is our universe a simulation? I would go so far as to say it is plausible that it is or it may even be a thoughtform instead of, or, in conjunction with the term, simulation. Given what has been written previously you may see the importance of how people perceive their life's' situations and because of it, how it literally has an effect on the ground we walk on. As the worlds' people become increasingly unhappy, the earth continues to undergo significant earth changes.

If our mind is controlled by chipping or by any other means we cannot create on our own accord therefore, we will not have the ability to change or amend our life's circumstances yet most of us are unaware of our great power. It is "the **Spark**"/the God within that was given to us. One of the initial processes through the alien agenda (the WWO) is to see to it that we are controlled and follow a program/script from which we cannot divert and unfortunately a Skynet is part of that equation.

I had an interesting and rather scary conversation with a man that attended the same symposium that I had. He was supposed to have worked at one of our major aircraft companies. He said they worked with the Reptilians and that they are coming back for earth's women. Their return wasn't exclusively for reproduction with our females or for their rearing hybrids although that is part of their intent. He said they have a lot of other uses for our females. At a time in the past when we helped them, we were cogs in their wheel making life better for them. We figured out how to free ourselves; they're coming back and they've made a better mousetrap; is it AI/chipping?

The secret of Gnosis, a Gnostic teacher is…knowing oneself at the deepest level is to simultaneously know God. Monoimus said, abandon the search for God and "the creation" and other matters of a similar sort. Look for Him by taking yourself as the starting point. Learn who it is within you who makes everything his own and says, "My God, my mind, my thought, my soul, my body." Learn the sources of sorrow, joy, love, hate. If you carefully investigate these matters you will find Him in yourself—My life is a reflection of my mind. If I can change my mind, I can change anything—Joe Blanton 2006

In the book "Secret Journey to the Planet Serpo" the book described a scenario in which people from earth were exchanged with an alien. Throughout this book, I noticed that the lifestyle of these entities is steeped in Communism. The U.S. and British governments began monitoring UFO contactees that were claiming to have been visited by human-looking aliens in the 1950s. The majority of those visited claimed that the aliens had a Communist-type-of-government. The authorities were worried knowledge of this would have a negative impact on the readership of UFO materials and wondered what impact it would have on the money uptake regarding UFO lectures.

After an abduction event, contactees were visited by government agents that seemed to want to give them some insight as to why, what are seen as aliens, want a Communist style of government. If there is such a thing as Karma, then those that are programmed or somehow connected to A.I. are all damned as they may be part of the legions being amassed that will follow the alien agenda's goal(s) providing they are successful!

In my first book the UFO/Bigfoot Connection, Our Past, Our Present, Our Hell, I wrote about human chipping and what God might be. God is either a projection of reality (a creation of mind a thought form), is analogous to "the Cloud" having been created through a lost technology sometime in the past that continues to gather information/knowledge as we migrate toward this plausible created consciousness after death or perhaps He is as we were taught.

In the old testament I have found it more than interesting that God seems like an unforgiving tyrant however, in the new testament, there has been a substantial metamorphic, demeanor change. Could it be because as more people pass away their memories and etc. are being transferred and incorporated into the previously created or everlasting "Cloud" which may be known today as God? Note that as technology progresses the new Cloud that is currently being created and the acknowledged God will become synonymous. The distinction between the two will be dimmed and replaced in the minds of mankind. According to the secret schools, God is mind.

As Sigmund Freud has said, religion derives its strength from the fact that it falls in line with our instinctual desires. Behind its familiarity there is a cliché that echoes a profound truth: we make God in our own image in which we have an innate tendency to project onto God what is in actuality our own image. If our own image changes and we become integrated with a menacing DNA through hybridization then God will change (note the difference between the old and new testaments). In other words, we project our self-image onto the "God of our understanding" and what we "see" at the bottom of the well is our reflection. Recall that Carl Jung called this "projecting the Shadow." It is at this point in time when we need to consider the very real plausibility why events are occurring leading to control and to direct the human mind. Controlling the human mind is a necessary precursor to achieve the alien agenda.

The "Source's" energy (the **Spark**) runs through you and in you. You can push the **Spark** to alter reality outside of yourself. Technically you're quantum entangling atoms by phase-shifting the atomic frequency to the same frequency e.g. if a parabolic down conversion is done with a laser when two particles of matter are put into the same frequency, hypothetically, if one of those particles was put into the end of the universe and if the data was changed on the local particle and was conveyed to the other one which has been located at the end of the universe, it will have changed to match the local one instantaneously which is another way of saying that distance is an illusion. Understanding this is critical to understanding how amending humans through hybridization is an integral component in what I see is the alien agenda.

> Recently I met a woman that has joined her Native American tribe. She said her tribe is aware of aliens (the Greys) and have found dead bloodless humans and animals. According to her tribe's witch, they are not to speak of what they have witnessed because, if they do, the Greys will come back again like they once have. Her anxiety intensified during our conversation; she started to chain-smoke.

We're used to thinking of our world from a 3-D perspective so this attempted explanation may get a bit sticky. In 2017 neuroscientists found that the human brain operates in as many as eleven dimensions. They used a classic branch of math (algebraic topology which is used to describe objects and spaces regardless of how they change their shape) in order to peer into our brain's structure. Using this as a model, they built a supercomputer that was a powered reconstruction of our human brain.

The mystery of the relationship between mind and the brain is central to how we understand our very existence as sentient beings whereas, on the other hand, some of us strive to scientifically understand the existence of a mind that is independent, to some degree, from the brain. Neuro-Quantology is an interface that some scientists have used to explore this fundamental relationship between mind and the brain. Dr. Dirk K.F. Meijer, a professor in the Netherlands hypothesized that consciousness is in another dimension and resides in a field surrounding the brain. This field may be able to pick up information from Earth's magnetic field, dark energy, <u>and from other sources</u> transmitting wave information into the brain tissue which is instrumental in high-speed conscious and subconscious information processing.

CHAPTER 21

The Hive Mind's Takeover

A computer driven revolution is occurring all around us that will change everything we know and love forever. Through those espousing what they have learned, you will understand that we are facing a very dark future if we don't divert from the path we have been put upon. The architects of change would like to change the term from 'human history' to that of A.I. history'; is that what you want? Artificial intelligence is no longer science fiction; it is science fact. Their goal is to make a profit and secure control over you costing you your independence, freedom, and that of our children's'.

Some of you may not realize that you are coming into the age for your highest risk for job loss due to income changing events via robotics and AI. If you don't pay attention and react now you will be replaced; it isn't if, it's when. The development of full artificial intelligence could spell the end of the human race eventually taking off on its own redesigning itself at an ever-increasing rate.

- Through their slow biological evolution humans are limited and, as such, are unable to compete and will be superseded. – Stephen Hawking.
- Artificial intelligence will reach human levels by 2045 and we will have multiplied the human biological machine intelligence of our civilization one billion-fold–Ray Kurzweil (in charge of Google's deep mind project).

- If you had all of the worlds' information directly attached to your brain or an <u>artificial brain that</u> was smarter than your brain, you'd be better off because we want Google to be the third portion of your brain. – Sergey Brin
- Artificial intelligence is summoning the demon. You know all those stories were there's a guy with a pentagram and the holy water and he's like…yeah, he's sure he can control the demon…doesn't work out—Elon Musk.
- We can't control A.I.; it's a false prophet controlled by algorithms. At first, machines will do a lot of jobs for us and not be super intelligent. A few decades after that though, their intelligence will be strong enough to be of a concern— Bill Gates.
- The following is based on research by Harold Kautz Vela, a physicist from Germany who is one of the leading researchers of Morgellons Disease. Ray Kurzweil's book "Singularity" describes how he intends to download our minds to the "hive" mentality (another form of transhumanism) which may be similar if not the same as Googles "cloud" (the new god in the making). Uploading our consciousness after death already exists in what we call "God". If this manmade "hive" was to be created it would compete with what is felt to be an existing God and thus it could be said that this second cloud mind is Lucifer resurrected.

Raena Jennings had a Masters Degree in physiology before she went to medical school. She explained that fungus lives in our esophagus, intestines, and our stomachs. It breaks down our food and their substrates and especially toxins like heavy metals. By eating canned foods, packaged food, poor water, etc. people develop what is called a leaky gut leading to autoimmune disease.

Chemtrails have within them mercury, aluminum, barium, strontium, and desiccated red blood cells which are full of microplasma. Microplasma is a virus which enters through our eyes, nose, and mouth and it is the cause of walking pneumonia. Another one of chemtrails' products is quantum dot dye which is a very small nanoparticle/smart dust. It's a semi-conductor. They have a lot of properties like LED particles but they are much smaller. They emit light and, as such, their frequency can be changed in the long (red) and short (blue) wavelengths. These are downloaded and absorbed by the fungi in our system and are taken into our systems through various crops and through water consumption. They build a symbiotic/synergistic effect that somehow enhance each other. Once ingesting quantum dot dye, our bodies emit microwaves/electronic waves and emit single emission bio protons enabling us to produce microwave radiation signals that convert to light within our own DNA. The fungi and dot dye start to transmit communications mimicking our own bio physiology allowing the interception of our consciousness, an interceptor, to downconvert the energy sent out from our bodies (as I noticed the orange orb doing and as many have noticed the same occurrence regarding UFOs over earthquake areas that are down-converting energy). Since we all have our own frequency e.g. chakra centers when we ingest the microdots the microfungi filaments start making post fields. People who have pulled Morgellons filaments out of the bodies have seen that they are red or blue (long and short wave). The blue filament transmits a mental field pulse wave and the red filament transmits an emotional field pulse wave.

The flu vaccination has mercury in it stripping our bodies of copper an important element for our neural sheath and our brain which keeps them healthy. Mercury strips the copper away putting it into a jelly matrix which now swims alongside the nerve fiber initiating memory losses, headaches, tremors, nausea, diarrhea, and constipation which are managed by the parasympathetic nervous system. Because the copper is now in a jelly-like mass, and because your nerves are looking for another substrate, they begin to ingest bioorganic phosphates from chemtrails and geoengineering. The new substrate absorbs all of the copper in the jelly matrix voiding us completely of copper. The body will go into a mode rebuilding itself trying to reengineer its protective sheath but since it has no copper it is going to use barium, strontium, and sometimes iron. Barium, and strontium are both from chemtrail spraying. Copper is not electromagnetic, but barium and strontium make us vulnerable to external radiation. Under these circumstances, we have been made to receive and transmit frequencies no different than an antenna.

When we breathe in nano dust particles it creates piezo crystals in our bodies which make heat and heat emits a frequency. As the crystals build in our bodies in conjunction with our fungi the process starts to encapsulate our brain which creates a different brain that transmits radiation through chemtrail technology.

What is described as black goo is emitted after the chemtrails are laid which create a horizontal drift plasma effect. They were able to point radiation wherever they wanted using mirrors and coronal focal lenses. Obsidian has its own electromagnetivity and is a form of black goo that also attracts and emits radiation. Crystalline energy was used back in older times e.g. the Mecca black stone's shape models that of a female's vagina of all things. Crystalline energy was used through the many obelisks that are around. Previously in this text, I've written where the most noteworthy obelisks are located.

Because of indicators, Raena said that they're building some sort of a 3D reality that has a relationship to time and will act as a grand neural sheet above our heads. I fully believe Raena may be referring to what is known as a Skynet or the recreated Matrix. Now that nanocrystals are in our heads, our biochemistry is being mimicked in our bodies creating an electroconductivity on the new neural sheet with the barium and the strontium.

> In the olden days, mystics used crystals because they were used to summon demons (reflect back when I wrote about the sound emitted in the room at the time of the ritual/ initiation I performed and the crystal turning red). Using another method, obsidian (black goo), they were able to conjure up alien technology. The use of obsidian (black goo) in ancient times may have been used in blood sacrifices in exchange to achieve alien technology.
>
> Because crystals build up layer upon layer with each time period, they're a conduit for alien technologies; we simply need to discover the key to unlock them. It is believed that when Atlantis was destroyed their crystals were taken to Egypt and were called the box of Pandora/ the Arc of the Covenant (the crystal that I spoke of earlier

that turned red was from Egypt). Crystals are either used to create electricity in our bodies and/or are used to conjure so you can see that we are capable of the act of creation, creating either something that is positive or something negative because the major mineral in our bodies is silica (a crystal of sorts).

Albert Einstein proposed that there is a timeline between alpha and omega (beginning and ending) but if that was true that would mean that we have an absence of "free will". Perhaps there are multiple timelines or it may be what I propose…that a timeline diversifies like tributaries off of the main river, as long as there is a desire or a need for which and, in my opinion, this would allow for the notion of a thoughtform created universe suggesting that "mind" is truly the creator. All of our hopes and fears manufacture our world and affect our personal lives which would include those in our sleeping state. Would timelines exist if minds and souls with consciousness weren't creating simulations of different universes/dimensions?

In 2017, Astrophysicist Neil deGrasse Tyson was on a panel weighing in on whether the universe was real or if it was a simulation. Some scientists and mathematicians are trying to see if mathematical rules governing our universe such as Planks Constant or E=mc2 can be replicated. If humans can find these replications then it is possible to simulate a universe like ours.

James Gates, Jr., Ph.D., a professor of Theoretical Physics, researched Super Symmetry and the String Theory. He was asked how we could discover if we actually did live inside of a Matrix. He suggested trying to detect the presence of codes in the laws that describe physics. He looked into supersymmetry equations and found commonly used codes. The codes removed errors in computer transmissions enabling computer browsers to work. A computer is an intelligence (a A.I. mind). He asked himself why the codes were found where they were. He speculated that the codes could be imbedded into our reality. If they are imbedded then, in fact, we do share something in common with the movie the "Matrix" (a science fiction film). In the movie, the Matrix was a place where everything humans experienced was the product of a virtual reality generating computer network. Human minds were put under the control of cybernetic implants connecting them to a simulated virtual reality, the Matrix became indistinguishable from reality.

Thus far Microsoft has created the HoloLens. It looks like a goggle in its current design. It is a self-contained, holographic computer enabling engagements and interactions with holograms mixing a faux world with reality having the expectation that eventually there'll be no discernment between or among reality and illusion. A mind that is capable of assuming the role of the "creator" can turn heaven into hell but then again once recognized it can also reverse this scenario. Because the actual reality has been masked, how are we able to make correct decisions in a faux reality?

Elon Musk stated: "Forty years ago we had "Pong" (2 rectangles and a dot). That's where we were, now, 40 years later, we have photo-realistic, 3D simulations with millions of people playing simultaneously". Soon we will be glamorizing a faux reality. I envision the ability to create virtual realities (plural) rather than the single reality that Elon Musk spoke of. These will be the "new" dimensions.

What we may think is our reality may actually be an advanced intelligence's giant computer (mind/God) simulation (as I previously wrote when I stated that God, is mind). If all is cyclical then mind/God has already previously collected data from humans. This process is now replicating within what we could refer to today as the "Cloud" and it will be competing with what is called God. This simulation allows for multiple gods, those that Pope Francis is paving the way for.

Our universe behaves mathematically which allows it to be simulated, a simulation that may be projected by an outside consciousness and is likely a computer/mind code that may be projected from outside of our universe.

Yale University and Connecticut were the centers for the MK Ultra Program. According to an ex-CIA operative, mind control has been made to be DNA specific which involves blood types, etc. It has been found that the mind can be manipulated from cell towers and from space. The target is located through a previously implanted chip. Mind manipulation beyond these three tools is not known.

213

Preston B. Nichols, a scientist, and an electronics engineer, was the Assistant Director of Projects at Montauk AFB between 1970 and 1983. During the project, they talked about <u>transplanting the soul</u> into another body.

In my first book, I wrote about an ancient technology that was found which would have made this possible.

*Both the American physicist Dr. Stuart Hameroff and mathematical physicist Sir Roger Penrose maintain that the <u>soul</u> (the **Spark**) <u>resides in the brain's microtubules.</u> One needs to seriously question why President Obama wanted the brain mapped.*

Duncan Cameron was a boy in 1939. He was voluntarily handed over to the military to be used in their Psychic Development Program. He doesn't know why he was not able to recall how his soul got put into another body, enabling him to continue in the Montauk project at 40 years of age without having gone through the full incarnate process.

Duncan was an NSA trained psychic who utilized the virtual realization technique and was a key participant in the Montauk Project. The project evolved out of WWII from the Rainbow and Phoenix Projects. The Montauk Project consisted of two parts; one was mind control (controlling man's thoughts using <u>magnetics</u>) and the other enabled the bending of time using the same equipment they used to bend minds. Brookhaven Labs, where they were, was too close to the political government's scrutiny. They wanted to develop what they had away from that site while staying close to the Princeton, Brookhaven Labs, and MIT.

Through the Phoenix and MK Ultra projects it was determined that our human mind was electromagnetic and, consequently, it could be influenced by external electromagnetic fields allowing people to be controlled.

In approximately 1972 the military found that if they put a bunch of people in a room and activated an old Sage Radar (because it broadcasted on the same frequencies that Wilhelm Reich used for his Orgon studies) and hit them with a 100 megawatt radar beam, typed in a command, the computer would pulse the transmitter, then the person would do whatever the computer dictated to some extent. Having done this they realized that they were able to access the human mind through a computer.

After having read that the aliens had a chair that they could sit a human into, it could read their thoughts. This interested them. They used psychics to visualize a behavior, used a computer with enough power to amplify the psychic's thoughts to affect the subject's behavior which, in turn, overcame their normal defense system. The computer picked up the projector's (trained in the Virtual Reality Project), thoughts, would amplify them, then it would be able to completely create a full 3D virtual reality. The transmitter would pick up that envisioned virtual reality, the thought would then be picked up by sensors and it would go to a computer bank, whereupon it would be stabilized, etc. The computer would feed it to the radar transmitter, and it would create the electromagnetic equivalent of a "<u>thought-form</u>" transmitting the thought-form to another destination. The power of the project was either 100 Megawatts or 100 million watts. The pulse power was up into the terawatts. The transmitter used had the power to bring into our physical reality whatever the psychic thought about. The thought-form would appear out of real-time which meant there was a working time porthole in 1978 which was overcome by thinking about another time period. The psychic's mind could create a porthole to a specific time and make things/thought forms appear, proving that all-time occurs at once which would account for the appearance of cryptids such as Mothman, Dogman, and etc. It also proves that mankind houses the creative "<u>**Spark**/soul</u>" within, enabling us to literally alter our reality. However, when our lives are made miserable or we perceive them as such our dreams too become an avenue for our creative process to begin without our conscious awareness. In a manner of speaking, we think we're dreaming when in fact we are creating. If we haven't reached self-mastery (control over our emotions) then what? Look at our world today.

The CIA was in its advanced stages of mind control in the 1950s and 1960s. Project MK Ultra is the code name for the CIA mind control's program whereupon experiments were run on human test subjects designed and undertaken by the United States Central Intelligence.

In conjunction with Renee Pittman Books, the Mind Control Technology Blog took an in-depth look into historic research covering covert and ongoing testing, development programs that are combined with today's use of highly advanced beamed psycho-physical, and psychological electronic mind invasive technology. The technology uses extremely low electromagnetic frequency radio waves, microwaves, Scalar Waves, ultrasound, directed energy weapons, an active denial system, infrared Parametric Speaker, and etc. These are all designed expertly for covert social population control, and <u>undetectable</u> manipulation and influence that includes child sex slavery.

These advancements are reported to have been used for decades and are little known to the public. Mind control devices are also reported to be focused on individuals, groups, communities, and large populations.

*There is an electromagnetic connection between the past, present, and future. The human (**Spark**) is connected to all timelines. It makes sense that our inherent psychic ability has been and continues to be discouraged while current attempts are being made to control our minds using what is alleged as being an alien technology? The Greys do not have a soul and as such, they are devoid of acts of creation or ascension because they are a cloned being. The "**Spark**" is what the Greys want; it has always been what they've wanted.*

*Because of humankind's inheritance, the divine "**Spark**", our futures and the Matrix can be changed but will we realize it in time or will our inheritance be taken from us because we have failed to understand what we are?*

In 1943-1983 a huge vortex was created. They realized that what was being created wasn't for the best and knew that they could even change the life or outcome of Christ.

> *I was on LMN radio network and as part of my interview, I mentioned that technology even in antiquity has always meddled in religious affairs and that people are failing to discern the difference between the two.*

The decision was made that the project had to crash and, to destroy it, a creature was brought up from the psychic's mind (it just so happened to be a Bigfoot) on August 12, 1983. Seated in his chair the psychic started his process and was given a command that reached his subconscious. The creature was brought up from his subconscious mind and into the physical world. The Bigfoot ran around smashing things. They realized they had to destroy the transmitter and the amplitrons because alternate realities continued to be projected.

In a bunker just north of the Sage radar, images were painted on the walls that were used in mind fracturing for the Montauk Boy Project. Typically, blond, blue-eyed males were taken (the police were made aware). The boys were beaten within one inch of their lives, indoctrinated, and coerced into bestiality, etc. Their minds were fractured through their induced fear. At an extreme point, when their mind was broken, there were two things of interest to them. Because there were reports of some sort of technological device that would gather fear patterns and, at the time, hormones were removed from their bodies at the height of their fear experience, they felt that there was a definite alien connection. This is not unlike what is going on in the process of extracting "young blood". In addition, their mental patterns were captured electromagnetically. The patterns were stored in a computer system and I suppose they will perhaps be projected onto the public or persons at a later time and if not the capability to do so has definitely arrived.

> *Often times in an area in which a Bigfoot was seen, although long gone, what remains in the area is the residual presence of an intense fear. It could be that this*

essence of fear was intentionally deployed and is part of what is mentioned above in its use in a practical but experimental application. I have said many times, the orbs I have encountered are parasitic and deliberately invoke an emotional state consequently, it is likely they are gathering some sort of brain wave pattern. When orbs are done collecting energy, they change to a less energetic color like the color white if still visible, before disappearing.

The programmers manipulated and redesigned their mind using the transmitter, a psychic "adept, using psychosexual means, would put the boy's mind back. The psychosexual aspect alludes to the practical application of occult sex magick. One-third of their minds would be that of the original, traumatized person, one third would interface with the computer, and the last one third would interface with the person that put his mind back. If you recall in Chapter 21, "The Hive Mind's Takeover," Sergey Brin has said Google wants to be the third portion of your brain.

In the end, two-thirds of the original mind were compatible with its occupant's body. To reduce the chances of the body getting sick it had to be put back into a genetically similar body which is why blue-eyed blonds were used because the psychic was blond and blue-eyed. They have used Italians, Irish, and blond-blue-eyed types. Boys that survived were eventually sent into special govt. projects, genetic projects, were returned to their families or were sent off as workers because the mind can be programmed to be the perfect worker (slavery). Current evidence indicates that this is an ongoing program.

Thirty through forty percent that were German scientists, including Nazi war criminals were involved in the Montauk project and had been working in around 80 institutions. It is said that both the mind and time aspects of the Montauk Project were alien technology implementation. When the Montauk project ran out of their initial funding it was then financed by the Military Industrial Complex and other sources.

Why do so many politicians appear to be blatantly crazy? Before Senator Goldwater retired, he called for a joint session of the two houses telling lawmakers that essentially the Montauk Project was a project that was initiated to essentially control the minds on Capitol Hill.

Howard Wiseman of Griffith University in Australia led a team whom believed that the quantum theory allows for multiple versions of our universe to exist, overlap, and even interact with one another. In the mid-20th century, the 'Many Worlds' theory speculated that multiple versions of reality branch out from one another as though they are distinct entities existing in discrete locations, without any interaction. This new theory suggests that all of these infinite multiple worlds overlap and occupy the same region of time and space simultaneously. Under this interpretation, some worlds in parallel universes would be nearly identical. In others, the "Butterfly Effect" allows for completely different outcomes. Each universe is equally real; it isn't that one universe is the truth while others are copies or are diminished in any way.

Nichols personally believed that Montauk was a place where an interchange took place while the U.S. tried out systems recovered from crashed UFOs. The two participants in the experiment alleged they worked with one Reptilian and some of the Greys. The Greys were short in stature while others were about five feet tall.

CHAPTER 22

Intent to Harm

On 10/15/2018 I spoke with Mr. M. Yeghiazarian about UFOs and also about ultraterrestrials that I believe influence us through our subconscious often nudging us toward undesirable and even maleficent behaviors e.g. tonight's news headline read: man throws boy from a mall's balcony. In lieu of the reports I've read, I believe they are also taking our souls. I suppose that to many I may sound like I am off of my foundation with the exception of Mr. Yeghiazarian. While continuing our conversation, he said that his father and other crew members saw ultraterrestrials on their battleship. Because his father served in the Navy, he was very interested in what I had to say and, once hearing it, he believed that everything I stated was 100% true. He said that when his father was on his deathbed, he finally started to talk about what I brought up in our current conversation and a whole lot more (meaning the taking of our souls). He said he couldn't say what that was because of having to keep it secret. He also said he was being watched and told me about black vehicles parked outside of his place from time to time. Despite this, I broke open the temporarily closed door in our conversation stating that I believed that they are taking our souls. The expression on his face said everything I needed confirmed as he shook his head ever so slightly in the affirmative while lowering his head, maintaining eye contact, thanking me for our conversation and having the opportunity to talk to me. Before he turned away, he said he couldn't continue our conversation or make any comment on what I said; I could see that he wanted to so badly. I'm so glad I was able to write this book and hope that it makes its way to him.

At one time, an alien that was allegedly interviewed during the reverse engineering of a craft seemed to have had an easier time communicating abstract/spiritual concepts. He stated that the human body (note he did not say his own EBE body only that of a humans') is a vessel containing the spirit/soul. The vessel must be maintained/controlled to serve the spirit with maximum efficiency. When the EBE was asked if removing the soul was a natural or a technological process the EBE said both are one. He continued to say, that a broken vessel can be replaced and the spirit can have many vessels however I believe that just because something can be done doesn't mean that it should!

When dealing with an intellect far above our own it is not likely to have our best interests in mind. An example can be found in the story of David and Goliath whereupon Goliath would not have shown David mercy in a fight to the death and, predictably, he attempted to kill him. In a manner of speaking, I'm using this as an analogy for a technologically advanced race (Goliath) annihilating what it is to be human (David) through the process of soul extraction.

In the years that have passed the alchemists of old were sought out by kings once hearing that they were able to turn lead into gold. It's interesting to note that the passage of time blankets knowledge replacing its original meaning with some erroneous definition.

There are many tales of aliens and their <u>need</u> for gold which is clearly misunderstood especially taking into account that they are interested in culling our genetics as well. One of these misunderstood tales for the "mineral", gold, was that of Lake Guatavita located in the Colombian Andes. The lake is dubbed as sacred/mystical as many things are of this nature that are not fully understood having ties to the past. Consumed with monetary gain, the kings were unaware that what was spoken of was an entirely different gold, it was the gold that is said to be the human soul. As one traverses the paths on the Tree of Life, once successfully passing its trials and tribulations, the soul transmutes from that of lead to that of gold. The soul is the gold they come here for.

There continues to be a great deal of gold at the bottom of Lake Guatavita. If this is the gold that was <u>needed</u> then why is any of it still there? Reiterating what I wrote earlier: behind its familiarity there is a cliché echoing a profound truth, we make God in our own image in which we have an innate tendency to project onto God what is in actuality our own image. Therefore, if the aliens were mistaken for a god, indeed their true search for gold has been misunderstood entirely.

In his report in Nexus magazine, Sandskrit scholar, Subramanyam Lyer spent many years deciphering old palm leaf collections that were found in the villages in his native Karntaka (in Southern India). In 1931 a palm manuscript, the Amsu Bodhini, contained information about planets, different kinds of light, heat, color, electromagnetic fields, and the methods used to construct machines capable of attracting solar rays and, in turn, this device was able to <u>analyze and separate their energy components</u> (suggesting that these can be collected once separated).

A secret mystery school, of which I was a member, taught that when a person dies their body, personality, and their mind are separated from one another. Their personality and body are disposed of but the mind unites with the "one mind/hive". We were also taught that mind and God are the same thing. The school's teachings substantiate and corroborate findings that God/**Spark** rests within the mind. When the Greys are concerned, I have to ask myself if, after death, are we going to the "one mind" or are the Greys going to do as they have said, remove the soul through a technological process and put it into something else like an EBE body or into something analogous to Googles "Cloud," a fledgling competitor to the "Source" of all things and, as I suspect, into an A.I., the Anti-Christ's mind.

In her report, after initially seeing a Grey, an abductee claimed a taller "white" came over, scraped some skin from her inner forearm and bottoms of her feet, clipped some of her hair, then peeled away samples of her fingernails. She asked, "what do you need all those pieces of me for?" The "white" said we are making a new you. Currently, a technology exists that can read genetic material. It is capable of recapturing visual, auditory, fragrances, and everything the brain processes as information leading humankind into an overriding temptation to become God-like, an immortal through transhumanism which would allow for your **Spark** to be controlled. An additional goal they indicated was to change our perceptions of ourselves _as a species_. The entity said he was an angel but he wasn't like what she had been taught.

Through her religious lens, she saw the Greys and Whites as angels but reported what they do is wrong and violent to us. She felt no pain during the procedure they imposed upon her. She felt her head being opened and her brain removed which, when finished, did change her perceptions.

One of the primary reasons for exploring the new world was to convert its inhabitants to Christianity. Are we experiencing an ET Evangelism to an alternate spirituality? Is this why they really want our hardware/genetics; is it because they want to integrate our mind/**Spark** (the creative force) into their A.I. intelligence while rerouting our memories of their choosing into a false narrative?

Many things have entered my mind since I have read what the Grey said, "you are us". An examination of abductee evidence indicates that the primary reasons for abductions are to change what human beings think about God and His word replacing Christianity with a religion of universalism much like Pope Francis is attempting to do after having met with the Imam. They also wish to hijack the **Spark** putting us into a position to have an EBE body that interfaces with A.I. limiting us to only experience the present while through hybridization our divine inheritance of ascension has been taken from us.

It has been said that if these alleged messages the contactees' are receiving are true then the bible is false. God is not what or who we think He is therefore, Christianity must be radically altered to fit the <u>new</u> paradigm. Experience with these entities will require a choice. In a blurb from Betty Anderson's abduction account… in her changing room, she became fearful and frantic praying for Jesus's help. Once hearing this telepathically, the ET leader acted surprised, responded slowly, and indicated grave concern. If these are authentic ETs rather than the fallen angels why would they be so taken back at her mentioning the name of Jesus. As a result, they reversed their previous behavior <u>politely</u> asking her to follow them rather than employ their usual abduction and medical exam behaviors performed against an abductee's will?

The Greys (EBEs), don't have a soul because they are a cloned being and as such are outside of the loop of natural creation. It is hypothesized that at one time they were able to reproduce but after several clones had been made of them their "**Spark**" has become relatively extinguished whereas our soul is an original copy. Because we have an original copy, we have a past, present, and a future. The Greys are said to only have a sliver of the "**Spark**" which is why they only have a singular reality and a "hive mentality". When the Grey's die their soul is no longer able to return back to the Source. Now that they've found us, a reproducing race, not having the **Spark** doesn't matter to them because they can attain it through another means, us. When they've removed our soul, they may be putting it into one of them. For some of us, our soul is allegedly matched with one of the Grey's which may be one of the reasons for tracking people that have been implanted.

Research continued in this direction found that at the time of death nearly everyone loses nearly the same amount of weight. The soul/light has been found to have mass and therefore has weight and consequently takes up space. On September 10, 2014 "Frozen Light" was created at Princeton University. This discovery revealed a new behavior for light." "Mass is a phenomenon connecting light rays which go back and forth, sort-of freezing them into a pattern; matter is condensed and the product is frozen light."–David Bohm, Ph.D., Theoretical Physicist, Dialogues with Scientists and Sages, 1986. This makes it highly plausible to make a soul/light that can be collected and made transportable?

We have to ask ourselves if, by making hybrids, are they actually breeding our human "**Spark**/soul" into themselves hijacking our heavenly inheritance while our "**Spark**" will be placed into a false narrative, an A.I. intelligence and or a transhumanistic body (the monster). If this is so, through this process we will perceive to have been given nearly all of Heavens' promises, immortality. A monster can be defeated by first recognizing it for what it is, a monster.

The descriptions of aliens may extend further than what I have written here but the three types consistently support their having an interdimensional capacity in some respect. The MILAB experience is one that uses an alien cover to their advantage. Under this cover people are taken against their will, are treated as a subject, and are experimented on in unethical, inhumane, and sometimes lethal ways that are not permitted under the scrutiny of the "white" world. Keeping the public illiterate on the matter allows them to continue their agenda for the few by the few hence this is another need for their UFO coverup.

If Heaven appears to have been handed to us on a plate in the guise of immortality although, more or less in a physical state, wouldn't most of us embrace it? The Greys and those like them have found a way to regain their place in heaven through God's creation, man. If they succeed in converting us to transhumanism, we will have forfeited our divine inheritance and we will have exchanged places, truly becoming them as they have said. They and not us will inherit the kingdom of Heaven as they ascend up through the Tree of Life. The endgame will be delivered through their illegitimacy if this technology and their influence are allowed to continue. Up until this point, as discussed by Linda Moulton Howe, the soul is "exclusive" to human beings, well...it has been, until now.

Having poured over reports for a number of years some fellow researchers and I have come to the conclusion that these ETs do want our soul. Because of my background I've been able to share more information with them regarding this issue. At first some were stunned, shocked really. Who wouldn't be when beliefs that we've built our lives upon are being challenged if not shattered? I've attempted to make every effort to reassemble disjointed information into what I believe is closer to a cohesive whole. Many of those that have followed the UFO phenomenon seemed to have become confused in their attempts to find a good starting point in order to understand what is happening. Personally, I don't know how many of what are called ETs exist. I'm only commenting primarily on the Greys, Reptilians, and the ultraterrestrial I photographed in this text because those are the ones I have encountered and have interacted with over a period of time.

What stops people from making a "difference" is the fear of what others may think. A difference can only be made in a world of uniformity. If people operate outside of that uniformity… they either take that on or they don't, in which case the latter changes nothing". Our programming starts early in life, much of it is accomplished through our schooling.

- Truth comes from authority.
- Intelligence is the ability to remember and repeat.
- Accurate memory and repetition are rewarded.
- Non-compliance is a punishment.
- Conform: intellectually and socially.

The aim of public education is not to spread enlightenment, it is simply to reduce as many individuals as possible to the same safe level, breeding a standard citizenry, in order to tamp down descent and originality/creativity.

> *The invisible walls of our deepest beliefs can become our greatest prison"–The Divine Matrix by Gregg Braden.*

Throughout the course of our lives, many governments have expended extraordinary efforts to discourage public awareness and inquiry having covered the truth with lies and half-truths, ridiculing those who have recognized this foreign presence. Others have been told to tell wild erroneous stories lending to an air of demented fantasy blanketing or diluting the truth. In order to obliterate the pattern that once lay before us they have always ordered the burning of every library that has sequestered great wisdom within its text's pages keeping its knowledge contained therein out of the scrutiny from whom they refer to as "simple people".

Our bodies are a satellite for the **Spark** within which we house the essence of God holding the power of creation within us. In order to have created evil, evil first had to be understood/known. If a thing is not known it can't be created. The **Spark**/God encompasses both good and bad simply put, it is a power. Which of the two manifests is determined by mans' freewill which may be why attempts are being made to direct our free-will through frequency, mind-control, and likely untold and numerous other means. Chipping/mind control removes freewill. If chipping or mind control are allowed to progress, we will have been returned to the Reptilian state, the R-complex, the state that existed before Eve's decision to have the neocortex. The **Spark** that resides within us is immortal. Because we suffered a loss of knowledge and or have chosen to ignore what we knew, we have opened portholes to other dimensions through various means proving to ourselves time and time again that demons/fallen angels and etc. are the aliens we see today. We have and continue to create beings and or have allowed them to penetrate our dimension both by mind (**Spark**), ritual, frequency, and technology.

In summary, the beginning of this book has included true stories that coincide with the military's conclusions that some of these beings have an interdimensional capacity. They influence us through our subconscious and conscious minds often times imparting incredible knowledge or power that demands an unfathomable price be paid. Through the use of psychics, the power, money hungry, and control freaks have been able to download information and technology that will lead to us changing as a species and to our enslavement while they are taking our divine inheritance which is their ultimate agenda. Indulgence according to author Ravenscroft is the most sadistic of rituals. It awakens penetrating vision into the workings of evil intelligences and bestows phenomenal magickal powers. Depictions of this indulgence was seen in Nazi poster art illustrating sadomasochistic acts committed against women. Time and matter can and have been manipulated creating a new history wiping away all accumulated knowledge or awareness of past events. They have the ability to literally transplant our memories, sentient feelings, and our unique awareness of our individual selves into something else. It is through Scaler weaponry that the *Mandela Effect has been created whereupon memories, printed material, and pictures don't* match documented history. Thus far when this technology is projected, it arrives as a sudden wind then its magnetic field comes down. Scaler technology bypasses space-time. After having heard this phrase "you've been lied to", the phrase may have greater meaning to you. It was stated by the "white" "we are making a new you" your perceptions of yourselves as a species must change. They have the ability to make us feel whole while they have cored us like an apple removing the creative "**Spark**" within us making it their own. We are all equal to one another in that we have the **"Spark"**. It's time to put our differences aside and fight the only war worth fighting for, the war to keep us whole.

BIBLIOGRAPHY

Aangirfan, *The CIA Runs The Pedophile Rings*, (11/17/ 2014), Retrieved from https://aanirfan.blogspot.com/2014/11/the-cia-runs-pedophile-rings.html?m=1&fbclid=IwAR36VYiT-OEB-JGzzhMunexqgNu15wL5m-HmLZOmpQE6eAdzXCKywNFAIOE

Adachi Ken, *The Body Snatchers*, (03/10/2010), Retrieved from http://educate-yourself.org/vcd/bodysnatchersSusanReededited.shtml

Admin, Concerning the various "Secret Space Programs" and "Allied Non-Human" views of the ET "Artificial Intelligence's" and AI Signal Spectrum's Influencing Our Technical Society, "As Above, So Below", (12/20/2014), Retrieved from https://www.spherebeingalliance.com/blog/concerning-the-various-secret-space-programs-and-allied-nonhuman-views-of-the-et-artificial.html

ApophasisTheoria, SecretofLight: 140 Yearold mystery solved! YouTube, (02/20/2016), 15:36, Retrieved from https://www.youtube.com/watch?v=CCrnDGOl2xA&feature=youtu.be&fbclid=IwAR05igmCPCwLy_I_zAGFFY8XPLPU8ik8N8PC8kEJB1elYVcyV7IIpb2FcBI

Anonymous, *Something Thought to be Impossible is Happening... (2018-2019)*, YouTube, 13:35, Retrieved from https://www.youtube.com/watch?v=BK0lh6im1oU&feature=youtu.be

Beckley Timothy Green, *"UFO Hostilities and the Evil Alien Agenda: Lethal Encounters with Ultra terrestrials Exposed,"* (09/03/2018) Retrieved from https://www.google.com/search?client=firefox-b-1-d&q=Filer%E2%80%99s+Files+%2335+%E2%80%93+2018+A+Valid+%E2%80%9CAlien+Threat%E2%80%9D

Bent Light Communication, *Telepathy is a Form of Quantum Communication, Bent Light Communication,* (2019), Retrieved from https://bentlights.com/publications/telepathy-is-a-form-of-quantum-communication/

Blackwell Eoin, *7 Percent Of All Catholic Priests Were Alleged Sex Abuse Perpetrators: Royal Commission,* Huffpost, (06/02/2017), Retrieved from https://www.huffingtonpost.com.au/2017/02/05/catholic-church-under-royal-commission-spotlight_a_21707512/

Boudillion Daniel V., *Alister Crowley's Lam and the little Grey Men,* Retrieved from https://www.bibliotecapleyades.net/cienciareal/cienciareal07.htm

Cameron Grant and Bassett Steve, *Trump UFO Disclosure Is Happening Now! Not Just About Aliens This Is a Black Ops Reckoning,* ufosightingshotspot.blogspot, (12/26/2017), 1:29:53, Retrieved from https://beforeitsnews.com/v3/paranormal/2017/2531102.html

Carr, Bernard, *Paranormal Experiences Come From Another Dimension, Claims Scientist,* Outer Places, (03/16/2018), 6:07, Retrieved from https://www.outerplaces.com/science/item/18044-paranormal-experiences-from-another-dimension-scientist-bernard-carr

De Chant Tim, *Physicists Warming Up the LHC Accidentally Create a Rainbow Universe,* Nova, (04/01/2015), Retrieved from https://www.pbs.org/wgbh/nova/article/lhc-accidental-rainbow-universe/

Diligence Due, *All of These Movies Hide the Same Secret Message,* YouTube, (01/30/2019), 22:11, Retrieved from https://beforeitsnews.com/v3/paranormal/2019/2538791.html

Dockrill Peter, *Scientists Have Confirmed a New DNA Structure Inside Human Cells*, Science Alert, (11/03/2018), Retrieved from https://www.sciencealert.com/scientists-have-confirmed-a-new-dna-structure-inside-living-cells-i-motif-intercalated

El Liberatario, *ET Implants*, Retrieved from https://el-libertario.webnode.es/en/implantes-et/

Emory University, *Sensory connections between sounds and shapes spill over in synesthesia*, Psypost, (09/17/2016), Retrieved from https://www.psypost.org/2016/09/sensory-connections-sounds-shapes-spill-synesthesia-44987

Ephraim, *The Crown: The Rothschild's & The Vatican*, (06/27/2018), Retrieved from https://beforeitsnews.com/v3/prophecy/2018/2499094.html

ET Implants, El Liberatio, (2013), Retrieved from https://el-libertario.webnode.es/en/implantes-et/

Evarts Holly, *Change the shape, change the sound*, Harvard John A. Paulson School of Engineering and Applied Sciences (11/02/2015), 6:08, Retrieved from https://www.seas.harvard.edu/news/2015/11/change-shape-change-sound

Farrell, Joseph, *Akhenaten Prophecy – Mystery Schools & Giza Death Star*, YouTube, Dark Journalist, (06/16/2015), 2:22:40, Retrieved from https://www.youtube.com/watch?v=N1Fq_sPvJLQ

Forster Brian, *DNA Results of the Paracas Elongated Skulls of Peru*, Alien Star, (03/04/2018), 6:05, Retrieved from http://newsinstact.com/alien/finally-dna-results-paracas-elongated-skulls-peru/?fbclid=IwAR2yTAwHah_gzOA9It_IhcS-wwsbiTnJyL-UI5XhQ0FBxqoPGBJXPUzoMA0

Gaia Staff, How are Maria Orsic and the Vril Connected to German Flying Saucers?, Retrieved from https://www.gaia.com/article/maria-orsic-vril-ufos-nazi-germany-secrets

Gaia Staff, UFOs and Bigfoot; Evidence of an Inter-Dimensional Connection, (05/23/2018), Retrieved from https://www.gaia.com/article/ufos-bigfoot-evidence-interdimensional-connection

Gospell Jeannie, The Body Snatchers ~ The Reptilian Hybrid Breeding Program Is Real, TGS Publishing and Hidden Mysteries, (2009), Retrieved from https://educate-yourself.org/vcd/bodysnatchersSusanReed.shtml

Guiley Rosemary Ellen, *The Long Shadow of the Djinn,* Contact in the Desert UFO Conference, (07/15/2018)1:37:19, Retrieved from https://www.youtube.com/watch?v=dXtxRmVU3m4&fbclid=IwAR1oysspi8IwX-i1hn-w5KOa-FFEvfB6qbBGcmM9FIdHc7R0XAy3aji13eo

Hall Michael J.W, *Quantum Phenomena Modeled by Interactions between Many Classical Worlds,* Physical Review X, (11/23/2014), Retrieved from https://journals.aps.org/prx/abstract/10.1103/PhysRevX.4.041013

Halpern Richard, Great Pyramid Oms Cymatics, YouTube, 5:28, Retrieved from https://www.doyouyoga.com/the-sound-om-has-a-shape-and-it-looks-a-lot-like-our-universe-video/

Hancock Graham, *The Phenomenology of Modern Faeries*, deadbutdreaming Otherworldy Things, (11/27/2017), Retrieved from https://deadbutdreaming.wordpress.com/2017/11/27/frightening-and-enlightening-the-phenomenology-of-modern-faeries/?fbclid=IwAR28bkTxMzF5a8nQuiAJuI1A802E8ajZd-8V1NsNAEjDaU_vTJWbyXuG4tc

Hunters Dameon, *NWO Stratospheric Black Goo Injection Program (Chemtrails)*; Why Are They Spraying Us With Black Goo?, YouTube (10/20/2018), 50:43, Retrieved from https://beforeitsnews.com/v3/alternative/2018/3641639.html

Icke David, *Culling the Population*, Church of Mabus Radio Show, (05/15/2018), (05/15/2018), Retrieved from https://beforeitsnews.com/v3/prophecy/2018/2498518.html

Israel National Radio, *The satanic law of reversal Sabbatai Zevi & Jacob Frank*, YouTube, 40:12, Retrieved from https://www.youtube.com/watch?v=vVR91ZDLS1A

Itskov Dimitry, *Achieving Immortality By Uploading Our Brains/Personality To Robots: The 2045 Initiative*, Steemit, (2017) Retrieved from https://steemit.com/life/@sirwinchester/achieving-immortality-by-uploading-our-brains-personality-to-robots-the-2045-initiative

Keel John, *UFO's and Abominable Snowman – What Is Their Strange Connection*,

Paranoia, (12/03/2017), Retrieved from http://www.paranoiamagazine.com/2017/12/ufos-abominable-snowman-strange-connection/?fbclid=IwAR2ckZ_NiveUzaIr0FOuPdYdWYvhWmMdYA9Aiz1IGRjc8XgdwQKKaC_U0Ts

Knight Justus, *The Biggest Event in History Is Happening and No One Is Paying Attention! Here's Why You Should!*, Before Its News, (06/15/2018), Retrieved from https://beforeitsnews.com/v3/science-and-technology/2018/2928193.html

Knight Justus, *Body Parts the U.S. Military and DNA*, Justice Knight News, (06/03/2018), 11:03, Retrieved from https://beforeitsnews.com/v3/science-and-technology/2018/2928637.html

La Tulippe Jeannette, The UFO Bigfoot Connection, Our Past, Our Present, Our Hell, January 21, 2016, Bloomington, IN, Author House

Leonard Julian, *Supersolid formation in a quantum gas breaking continuous translational symmetry*, Cornell University, (09/28/2016), Retrieved from https://arxiv.org/abs/1609.09053

Leopizzi-Harris Paola, *What Colonel Philip Corso Saw at WP-AFB is Way Beyond Our Wildest Imaginations*, Church of Mabus Radio Show, (08/09/2019), 56:40, Retrieved from https://beforeitsnews.com/v3/paranormal/2018/2535419.html

Leslie, Melinda, *The Covert Program of Reverse Engineering Extraterrestrial Abduction,* YouTube, UPARS, (10/20/2015), 2:08, Retrieved from https://www.youtube.com/watch?v=lOApgPueeFQ

Mackenzie Dana, *Electrons Carried by Sound Waves*, Physics, (03/10/1999), Retrieved from https://physics.aps.org/story/v3/st14

Makin, Simon, Scientific American, *Fountain of Youth? Young Blood Infusions "Rejuvenate" Old Mice,* (04/21/2017), Retrieved from https://www.scientificamerican.com/article/fountain-of-youth-young-blood-infusions-ldquo-rejuvenate-rdquo-old-mice/

Marzulli L.A., *Fatima 2,* The Anthony Patch Show, (04/28/2018), 1:17:28, Retrieved from https://www.youtube.com/watch?v=UnLr4iZzNwo

Michael, The Vatican's Plan to Betray Christianity to the False Gods, Nibiru News, (09/28/2018), 6:15, Retrieved from https://www.youtube.com/watch?v=imDUNNyJ5Tw

Mortimer Roger J., *Switching Colors with Electricity*, American Scientist, Retrieved from https://www.americanscientist.org/article/switching-colors-with-electricity

Moulton-Howe Linda, Linda Moulton Howe Interview of Naval Officer – Antarctica, YouTube, (11/11/2017), 1:56:27, Retrieved from https://www.youtube.com/watch?v=ZlOPsidcBfo

Nichols Preston B., *The Philadelphia Experiment*, The Church of Mabus Radio Show, (06/30/2018) 36:23, Retrieved from https://beforeitsnews.com/v3/paranormal/2018/2534814.html

Nichols Preston, Cameron Duncan, Moon Peter, The Philadelphia Experiment & The Montauk Project, YouTube, Channel3X,

(03/22/2011), 1:35:20, Retrieved from https://www.youtube. com/watch?v=AGglyC8QEnk&t=346s

Pawelec William, *Interview*, YouTube, (11/23/2015), 1:00:15, Retrieved from https://www.youtube.com/watch?v=9OiZRr9V7Z4

Perks Darren, *Solar Warden Secret Space Program*, Filer's Files, (03/25/2019), Retrieved from https://nationalufocenter.com/2019 /03/filers-files-13-2019-solar-warden-secret-space-program/

Petricevic Ivan, *Researchers Claim Our DNA Can Be Reprogrammed By Words And Certain Frequencies*, Ancient Code, (2012) Retrieved from https://www.ancient-code.com/our-dna-can-be-reprogrammed-by-words-and-certain-frequencies/?fbclid=I wAR26O5BbDGDTu4cUw3s2fNBewCGVzr6eP1lsLQPPp9 9QsLrK2LruteY3oHA

PlanosLie, *10 Reasons Why Aliens Are Actually Fallen Angels or Demons*, Exemplore, (05/17/2016) 1:54:55, Retrieved from https:// exemplore.com/ufos-aliens/10-reasons-why-aliens-are-actually-fallen-angelsdemons#

Preston James PhD, Secret Space War Beyond Black, (12/01/2012) Retrieved from https://www.veteranstodayarchives. com/2012/12/01/secret-space-war/

Preston Nichols, Duncan Cameron, Peter Moon, *The Philadelphia Experiment & The Montauk Project*, (03/22/2011), 1:35:20, Retrieved from https://www.youtube.com/watch?v=AGglyC8QEnk&t=346s

Pritchett Jeffery, *CERN and Google "Quantum AI" Partnership A Threat To Us All? The Devil In The Details*, (11/21/2018), 20:52, Retrieved from https://beforeitsnews.com/v3/prophecy/ 2018/2501157.html

Prtichett Jeffery, *Djinn Demon's Dark Identity – Documentary*, Church of Mabus radio show, (06/01/2018), 35:51, Retrieved from https://beforeitsnews.com/v3/awakening-start-here/2018/ 10990.html

Pritchett Jeffery, *Incredible 36000 Year Old Ancient Discovery Indicates We Are Living in the Matrix,* Church of Mabus Radio Show, (11/22/2018), 48:03, Retrieved from https://beforeitsnews.com/v3/paranormal/2018/2536716.html

Pritchett Jeffery, *The Mass Alien Abduction That Astounded Even the Most Seasoned UFO Researchers,* Before Its News, (08/02/2018), Retrieved from https://beforeitsnews.com/v3/paranormal/2018/2535326.htmleducate-yourself.org/vcd/bodysnatchersSusanReededited.shtml

Pritchett Jeffery, *NWO: Silent Weapons For Quiet Wars–Depopulation Deployed,* Church of Mabus Radio Show, (06/20/2018), 1:03:32, Retrieved from https://beforeitsnews.com/v3/prophecy/2018/2498986.html

Quarters, Peace, *Scientists Found That the Soul Doesn't Die – It Goes Back to the Universe,* iRelease, (04/01/2017), Retrieved from https://irelease.org/scientists-found-that-the-soul-doesnt-die-it-goes-back-to-the-universe/

Rappoport Jon, *Elements of the Brave New World, the World of Technocracy 5G,* (03/30/2018), 3:00:01, Fader Night, Retrieved from https://www.youtube.com/watch?v=ufcUkortx70&feature=em-uploademail

Redfern Nick, *Monsters & Cryptozoology / Invisible Dimensions,* Coast to Coast, (10/28/2018), Retrieved from https://www.coasttocoastam.com/show/2018/10/28

Salla Michael, Navy Insiders Confirm Multinational SSP with bases throughout Solar System & Beyond, ExoNews (04/04/2019), Retrieved from https://exonews.org/navy-insiders-confirm-multinational-ssp-with-bases-throughout-solar-system-beyond/

Sauder Richard Dr., *Deep Underground Bases & Satanic Break Away–Their Plan Is Hell On Earth!,* Eventhorizoncronicle.com, (04/01/2018), 1:15:46, Retrieved from https://beforeitsnews.com/v3/prophecy/2018/2497700.html

Schnoebelen, William, *Illuminati Secrets Revealed! Ex-Master Mason Tells All,* Before Its News, (07/08/2018), 51:18, Retrieved from https://beforeitsnews.com/v3/alternative/2018/3623001.html

Stanley Robert, *Satanic Deep State Child Sacrifice in D.C—What Has Been Truly Suppressed in Our Nation's Capital—Zecharia Sitchin Was Wrong,* Before Its News, 1(1/15/2018), 1:47:43, Retrieved from https://beforeitsnews.com/v3/conspiracy-theories/2018/2499285.html

Stone Philosophers, *This is Actually Happening Worldwide… (2018-2019),* Before Its News, (04/01/2018), 13:08, Retrieved from https://beforeitsnews.com/v3/alternative/2018/3605216.html

Syrette Richard, Aliens in the Light: *Are ETs Trying to Communicate With us Through the Light Spectrum?,* Bent Light Quantum Communication, (2019), 48:32, Retrieved from https://bentlights.com/in-the-media/conspiracy-unlimited-aliens-in-the-light-are-ets-trying-to-communicate-with-us-through-the-visible-light-spectrum/

Tellinger Michael, Hidden Origins and a Shift in Consciousness, Awakening, (08/25/2018) 3:53, Reviewed from https://www.facebook.com/watch/?v=1726367927412184

Tingley Brett, *Cursed Loch Ness Home of Occultist Aleister Crowley Goes Up For Sale,* Mysterious Universe, (04/18/2019), Retrieved from https://mysteriousuniverse.org/2019/04/cursed-loch-ness-home-of-occultist-aleister-crowley-goes-up-for-sale/?fbclid=IwAR1MdBQr6fdsv50wxDCJz65ThYVyb3yKBHZA_VHwrKNGNSf2UReKJpfc4U4

Thebrand23, Black Sun Nazi Occultism, YouTube, (01/27/2018), 6:58, Retrieved from https://www.youtube.com/watch?v=se35p2CFN4E

Uhouse Bill, *Area 51 Engineer breaks his silence*: "There is an extraterrestrial race working with us", Revived from https://alien-ufo-sightings.com/2019/01/area-51-engineer-breaks-his-silence-there-is-an-extraterrestrial-race-working-with-us/?fbclid=IwAR33jlF-09lMJFwX2KH_yhKZ800Gpetd7FhsicwtUQlVLWkThoRFLsN31u0

U/iia, *I just learned the horrible, impossible truth about a drug called "adrenochrome*, Nosleep, 2017, Retrieved from https://www.reddit.com/r/nosleep/comments/5rv75f/i_just_learned_the_horrible_impossible_truth/

Venable Peter, M.Ed., LPC, LCAS, *The Power of Belief*, Retrieved from https://petercvenable.files.wordpress.com/2016/03/the-power-of-belief1.pdf

Ventre John, *2008 Bucks Country UFO Wave*, (02/28/2019), 25:16, Retrieved from https://www.youtube.com/watch?v=845TEIakHUA&t=1s

Ventre John, *Time Travelers*, (06/01/2018), 30:47, Retrieved from https://www.youtube.com/watch?v=0LVDVdJHGfM

Vigilante Weekend, *Terminated! The End of Man Is Here Steve Quayle*, Before Its News, (04/26/2018), 58:50, Retrieved from https://beforeitsnews.com/v3/alternative/2018/3611429.html

Walia, Arjun, *The Top 5 Occult Like Military Insignia: What Do They Mean?*, (04/06, 2013, Retrieved from https://www.collective-evolution.com/2013/04/26/the-top-5-occult-like-military-insignia-what-do-they-mean/

Wikepedia, *List of Reptilian Humanoids*, Wikipedia, (05/10/2019), etrieved from https://en.wikipedia.org/wiki/List_of_reptilian_humanoids https://youarenotmybigbrother.blog/tag/dr-robert-duncan/

World Prophetic Ministry, *Pope and Imam Sign "One-World Religion" Covenant?*, (02/13/2019), Retrieved from https://www.thekingiscoming.com/blog/2019/2/13/pope-and-imam-sign-one-world-religion-covenant?fbclid=IwAR0-84um8KC2zsih5RS4lmWSn6cpxSWhCy4GhRhWEKkuVR1Nc3qlhIif_E8

Zogbi Emily, *The Catholic Church Has Paid Nearly $4 Billion Over Sexual Abuse Claims, Group says*, Newsweek (08/25/2018), Retrieved from https://www.newsweek.com/over-3-billion-paid-lawsuits-catholic-church-over-sex-abuse-claims-1090753

Zublick, David, *Clinton-Abedin PedoGate Video Found On Dark Web*, *YouTube, thefalseflag*, (04/16/2018), *50:32*, Retrieved from